Winner of the Bram Stoker Award for Non-fiction

Winner of the Halloween Br̶ ' ̶

'Well-written and illustrated, i̶
– *Fortean*

'If you want to know anything at all about the subject, you ought to find it in *Trick or Treat* ... Morton's interesting account of Hallowe'en is at its best when it comes up to date and there are many entertaining illustrations.
– SUSAN HILL, *The Times*

'*Trick or Treat* covers the history of Halloween from its ancient Celtic roots to its stunning growth in global popularity in the 21st century. Morton is an accomplished horror short story writer, and her ability to draw readers in quickly and keep them turning the pages shines through in her nonfiction as well. Lavishly illustrated, this solidly researched and concise work is fun to read and a great choice for readers who want to know why we seek out the scary each October.'
– *Library Journal*

'Morton offers the first comprehensive history of the 'misunderstood festival' of Halloween. She playfully sets the record straight on the origins of Halloween, explores its migration from the Old World to the New and back again, discusses the role of consumer culture in establishing supposedly ancient traditions, and concludes with an observation that Halloween's ever-changing nature has allowed it to be adapted for countless purposes around the globe ... This book is an excellent example of the scholarship on holidays as a means of accessing many facets of history. Highly recommended.'
– *Choice*

trick or treat

trick or treat

a history of halloween

LISA MORTON

REAKTION BOOKS

Published by
Reaktion Books Ltd
Unit 32, Waterside
44–48 Wharf Road
London N1 7UX, UK

www.reaktionbooks.co.uk

First published 2012

First paperback edition 2013

This edition published 2019, reprinted 2019, 2021, 2022

Printed and bound in Great Britain
by Clays Ltd, Elcograf S.p.A.

A catalogue record for this book is available from the British Library

ISBN 978 1 78914 158 0

Contents

Halloween jack-o'-lanterns.

Introduction

Halloween is surely unique among festivals and holidays. While other popular calendar celebrations, including Christmas and Easter, have mixed pagan and Christian traditions, only Halloween has essentially split itself down the middle, offering up a secular or pagan festival on the night of 31 October and sombre religious observance on the day of 1 November. As with Valentine's Day, many of those who celebrate Halloween are unaware of its Catholic history or meaning; but while Valentine's Day has remained recognizably the same for at least a century, Halloween has transformed over and over again. What began as a pagan New Year's celebration and a Christian commemoration of the dead has over time served as a harvest festival, a romantic night of mystery for young adults, an autumnal party for adults, a costumed begging ritual for children, a season for exploring fears in a controlled environment and, most recently, a heavily commercialized product exported by the United States to the rest of the world.

Halloween also has the unenviable distinction of being the most demonized of days: Christian groups decry it as 'The Devil's Birthday', authorities fear its effect on public safety and nationalist leaders around the world denounce its importation for conflicting with their own native traditions. Some of these concerns may be valid, but they are all rooted in a history that compounds confusion and error with occasional fact. Perhaps because Halloween has always been connected with the macabre, those who have chronicled it in the past have frequently been less interested in accuracy than in dramatic and ghoulish ramblings.

Despite a history extending back well over a millennium, it's only been within the last three decades that historians, folklorists and writers have begun to take the study of Halloween seriously. Even in that brief period of time, the day's identity has shifted, making it difficult to produce a comprehensive and up-to-date overview. Within the last year alone, Halloween has expanded into parts of the world where it was previously unknown, and in its main home, America, industries spawned by Halloween are starting to move beyond mere October celebrations. Halloween is truly becoming more than just a (mostly American) mark on the calendar; it's on the verge of blossoming into a global subculture.

Trick or Treat: The History of Halloween is the first book to look at both the history of the festival and its growth around the world in the twenty-first century. As such, it will hopefully serve to fill a gap in the understanding of Halloween, and to capture as detailed an image as possible of where it stands at this time – because, given the astonishing speed with which the festival continues to transform and expand, it's an image that will undoubtedly change again soon.

Halloween: The Misunderstood Festival

In 1762, British military engineer Charles Vallancey was sent to Ireland on a surveying mission. Vallancey, however, was no ordinary engineer: he was extraordinarily well-read in history and linguistics, corresponded with many of the leading proponents of the then-fashionable Orientalism and fancied himself a scholar and writer. He soon developed an obsession with the lore and language of Ireland's ancient Celts, and he wrote hundreds of pages of collected fact, observation and speculation on the green isle's early inhabitants.

There was just one problem: much of what Vallancey recorded was wrong.

By 1786, when Vallancey published the third volume of his opus *Collectanea de Rebus Hibernicis*, it was already well established that the name 'Samhain' (pronounced 'sow-in') referred to the three-day Celtic New Year celebration that began when the sun went down on 31 October. Other linguists had recorded the translation of 'summer's end' for Samhain, but Vallancey believed this was a 'false derivation', and went on to state that Samhain was actually a Celtic deity who was also known as 'BALSAB ... for *Bal* is lord, and *Sab* death'.[1]

It didn't seem to matter much that the name 'Balsab' appears nowhere else in Celtic lore, or even that Vallancey's work was dismissed during his lifetime (the Orientalist scholar Sir William Jones said of Vallancey, 'Do you wish to laugh? Skim the book over. Do you wish to sleep? Read it regularly'[2]). Somehow Vallancey's work found its way onto library shelves all over Britain, and formed a

Romanticized image of a Druid sacrifice, *c.* 1880.

strange alternate history of Samhain (and its descendant Halloween) that ran alongside the traditional Celtic folklore texts and
Irish dictionaries that defined the word correctly. Nearly two
centuries after Vallancey first journeyed to Ireland, books like
Halloween Through Twenty Centuries (1950) were still referring to

'Samhain, Lord of the Dead'.[3] By the early 1990s, Christian groups throughout America were urging parents to keep their children from celebrating a holiday during which 'human beings were burned as an offering in order to appease and cajole Samhain, the lord of Death'.[4]

How is it possible that religious and community leaders would use the writings of a romantic who was denounced in 1818 as having written 'more nonsense than any man of his time' in order to denounce a major celebration?[5] How could the history of what has become, in America at least, the second most popular holiday of the year be so little known?

Halloween is undoubtedly the most misunderstood of festivals. Virtually every English-speaker in the world can instantly tell you where the name 'Christmas' comes from – they could probably also provide an anecdote about St Patrick and his Day, and of course those celebrations with simple declarative titles, like New Year's or Father's Day, require no great linguistic skills – but amazingly few understand so much as the origin of the name 'Halloween'. The word itself almost has a strange, pagan feel – which is ironic, since the name derives from 'All Hallows' Eve'. Prior to about AD 1500, the noun 'hallow' (derived from the Old English *hálga*, meaning 'holy') commonly referred to a holy personage or, specifically, a saint.[6] All Saints' Day was the original name for the Catholic celebration held on 1 November, but – long after 'hallow' had lost its meaning as a noun – the eve of that day would become known as Halloween.

Halloween owes part of its legacy of confusion and obfuscation to those same Celts who provided the basis for the celebration with their Samhain. Surprisingly little is known of them since they kept no written records. Our knowledge of Ireland's Celts is based largely on orally transmitted lore (much of which was recorded by Christian monks of the first millennium) and scattered archaeological evidence. It's no wonder that writers like Vallancey – the ones with a more exotic take on history – dreamt of a race of savages who offered up human sacrifices to demonic gods and spent the autumn warding off evil spirits by constructing huge, roaring bonfires. By the mid-twentieth century, Halloween historians had added another mistake to their understanding of the day, stating that it was based in part on a Roman festival called Pomona, when in fact there was no such celebration. In the 1960s, a veritable cult of urban legends built up around Halloween – especially the notorious 'razor blade in the apple' myth, which suggested that innocent young children were at risk during the beloved ritual of trick or treat – although there were no recorded instances of real cases behind these modern myths. Over the next few decades, there were reports of anonymous psychos poisoning candy, costumed killers stalking college dorms on Hallow-een night and Satanic cults offering up sacrifices of black cats, and warnings of gangs initiating new members by committing murders on 31 October. It sometimes seems as though the prank-playing and mischievousness that have been a key factor in Halloween cele-brations for hundreds of years have crossed over and played tricks on its history.

The unassailable facts of Halloween are fourfold. First, it boasts both a pagan and Christian history. Second, its position in the cal-endar – at the end of autumn/beginning of winter – means it has always served in part as a harvest celebration. Third, it is related to other festivals of the dead around the world, and so has always had a sombre, even morbid element. Finally, however, its combination of pagan New Year celebration and joyful harvest feast have also given it a raucous side, and it has almost always been observed with parties and mischief-making.

Samhain and the Celts

Any examination of Halloween's history and its long line of mis-understandings must start by examining the Celts, an ancient people who themselves are often the subject of mistaken identity. The Celts were referred to as *Keltoi* by Greek and Roman writers (and probably by themselves), and it's likely that the name derives from the Indo-European word for 'hidden' (*kel-*), making the Celts literally 'the hidden people'. They once spread across most of Europe and throughout the British Isles, and they even occupied

Rome for several months around 400 BC. Many of Vallancey's contemporaries painted a picture of the Celts and their Druid priests that made his notions seem serene by comparison, as in this spectacular example from 1793:

> This degenerated priesthood seem to have delighted in human blood: and their victims, though sometimes beasts, were oftener men. And not only criminals and captives, but their very disciples, were inhumanly sacrificed on their altars; whilst some transfixed by arrows, others crucified in their temples, some instantly stabbed to the heart, and others impaled in honor of the gods, bespoke, amidst variety of death, the most horrid proficiency in the science of murder.[7]

However, contrary to the romantic notions of both ancient historians – including Julius Caesar – and later writers, the Celts were far from being warmongering primitives whose Druids were bloodthirsty slayers. Modern archaeological evidence as well as written historical remnants suggests that the Celts were skilled in mining and working with metals, farming, road-making, legal

'Frenzied Religious Orgies of the Druids'.

13

systems and medicine. Their religion involved hundreds of deities and barred written records of their rituals and stories, but some histories and various inscriptions made in Greek, Latin and, later, Irish, have survived and make up most of what we know about their celebrations and festivals. The Celts did engage in human sacrifice, but often chose the victims from within their own tribes by drawing lots in the form of bits of cake – whoever received the piece with the blackened bottom was offered to the gods to ensure the fertility of the herds, a fruitful harvest or victory in battle. The number three figures prominently in Celtic beliefs – many of their gods and goddesses were depicted with three heads or aspects – which is possibly one of the reasons why so many later Halloween fortune-telling games required a task to be performed three times. They believed in an afterlife, with souls journeying to an Other-world sometimes called *Tir na tSamhraidh*, or 'Land of Summer' (note the similarity to 'Samhain'). They believed that the doors between this world and that Otherworld opened one night a year – Samhain, of course. On that night, the dead might return to the living, and creatures called *sidh*, or fairies, could cross over to bedevil humans.

Samhain features frequently in Celtic lore. In practical terms, it was the end of summer and so the beginning of winter. Crops were gathered and livestock were brought in from the fields. Pigs and cattle were slaughtered, with only a small number kept for breeding stock. A Celtic day began when the sun went down, and so Samhain started with the onset of darkness on 31 October, with a feast celebrating the recent harvest and temporary abundance of food. Some archaeological evidence suggests that Samhain may have been the only time when the Celts had ready access to an abundance of alcohol, and the surviving accounts of the festival – in which drunkenness always seems to occur – support this as well.

Samhain was also an important day for administration, akin to the u.s. Tax Day in modern times. A yearly gathering was held at Tara, the ancient seat of kings, where three days' worth of feasting and sporting alternated with debt repayment and trials (those who were found guilty of particularly severe crimes were executed then as well).

Before the eve of Samhain, all home hearth fires were extinguished, and the Druids used 'needfire', or fire created by friction, to construct a bonfire on the nearby hill of Tlachtga; embers from this fire were distributed to each household, and a tax was exacted for this service.

But Samhain wasn't just a time of debts, livestock and feasting. It was also – with Beltane, or 1 May – one of the two most important days in Celtic heroic tales, which almost invariably contain some frightening element. In one early story, the Fomorians, a race of demonic giants who have conquered Ireland after a great battle, demand a yearly tax of two-thirds of the subdued survivors' corn, milk and children, to be paid each year on Samhain. The Tuatha de Danann, a race of godlike, benevolent ancestors chronicled in Celtic mythology, battle against the Fomorians for years, but it takes the Morrigan, a mother god, and the hero Angus Og to finally drive the monsters from Ireland – on Samhain, of course.

Samhain could have a romantic side as well, as attested to by a later story involving Angus. In 'The Dream of Angus Og', Angus is visited in his dreams every night for a year by a beautiful young girl with whom he falls in love. When she stops appearing to him, Angus begins to waste away until his father, the Celtic god the Dagda, goes to the *sidh* for help in finding the girl. After two years she is located among 150 other maidens who all bear silver chains. She is Princess Caer, daughter of King Ethal; the King, however, refuses to hand her over to Angus, and so the Dagda and his allies destroy Ethal's palace. It is only then that Ethal reveals the strange truth about his daughter: she has been bewitched, spending one year in human form and the next as a swan, transforming each Samhain. Angus goes to visit her in her swan form, and he changes himself into a swan so they can fly away together.

Halloween's sinister aspect is presaged in another traditional Celtic tale, that of the boy hero Finn mac Cumhaill, who journeys to the yearly Samhain gathering at Tara, presided over by the High King. The King soon puts a challenge before the rugged assemblage: each Samhain, a man of the *sidh*, Aillen, comes to Tara playing a harp that places all those who hear it under an enchanted sleep; Aillen then issues a wall of flame from his mouth and burns down the palace. Aillen has destroyed Tara nine times, and this year the King offers a reward to anyone who can stop him. Finn undertakes the task, and an ally gifts him with an enchanted spear. Finn uses the head of the spear to ward off the magical music and his cloak to turn aside the flame. Aillen tries to flee, but Finn casts the spear just as Aillen is stepping through the entrance to the Otherworld, and the *sidh* warrior is slain. Finn cuts off Aillen's head and returns it to the King the following morning, at which point he receives his reward.

Perhaps the most famous and eeriest Samhain story is 'The Adventure of Nera', in which the eponymous hero is challenged by King Ailill to place a loop around the foot of a hanging corpse on Samhain. Nera succeeds, and the corpse promptly begs him for a drink, claiming to have been thirsty when he was hanged. Nera removes the dead man from the gallows, and tries to find a house where he can treat the corpse to a drink; when he does, the corpse spits the drink back at the humans who are present, and they immediately die. Nera returns the corpse to the gallows and journeys back to Ailill's fort, only to find it engulfed in flames set by a fairy army. He follows the army back through their mound, and finds himself in the Otherworld. He takes a fairy wife there, who tells him that the fire was a hallucination but will actually happen unless he can warn Ailill. Returning to our world, Nera finds that no time has passed (a common theme in later Halloween tales is how time passes differently in the fairy realm), and he warns Ailill, who manages to destroy the malevolent *sidh* before they can attack again. Nera, however, spends the rest of his life in the Otherworld.

Although historians have argued over how much Samhain really contributed to the modern celebration of Halloween, it seems likely that the Celtic festival's peculiar mix of harvest, rowdy celebration and fearful supernatural beliefs gave Halloween much of its character. Just as Celtic culture was recorded by later Christianized Irish scribes, so those same Irish integrated aspects of their ancestors' Samhain into their own All Saints' Day – an integration that would prove an uncomfortable mix to the very Church that initially promoted it.

All Saints' and All Souls' Day

By the seventh century, the Catholic Church had spread through-out most of Europe; missionaries – including St Patrick, who would become the patron saint of Ireland – had successfully converted the pagan Celts. The Church had found that conversion was far more successful when attempts were made to offer clear alternatives to existing calendar celebrations, rather than simply stamping them out. Pope Gregory I (who would later be canonized) famously wrote a letter in 601 to an abbot en route to Britain, suggesting that exist-ing temples and even sacrificial rituals should not be destroyed but rather turned to use for Christian purposes. This doctrine, known as syncretism, even replaced lesser pagan gods with Catholic saints.

In 609, the Church put syncretism into action by converting the Pantheon in Rome to the service of the Virgin Mary and all the martyrs. The famed pagan temple was rechristened the Santa Maria Rotunda on 13 May of that year, and the forerunner of All Saints' Day was born. The choice of 13 May was important as well, since it had formerly marked the final night of Lemuria, a Roman festival of the dead. Like Samhain, Lemuria was celebrated over three nights, and was a time when the dead returned to the world of the living; however, the ghostly visitors of Lemuria (the *lemurs*) were terrifying creatures who were ritually expelled from the household at midnight on 13 May. The Romans also celebrated the spirits of their ancestors during Parentalia and its closing ceremony, Feralia, which took place on 22 February (and which later became the Catholic feast of St Peter).

One holiday the Romans did *not* celebrate (and which has become the source of historical misinformation) was a festival in honour of Pomona, a minor goddess of fruits and orchards. A contemporary of Vallancey's by the name of William Hutchinson may have started the error when he stated in 1776: 'The 1st day of November seems to retain the celebration of a festival to Pomona, when it is supposed the summer stores are opened on the approach of winter.'[8] Hutchinson was probably taking inspiration from poetry; the mythological tale of Pomona and Vertumnus was much in vogue in the eighteenth century thanks largely to Alexander Pope's translation of the story from Ovid's *Metamorphoses*, in which Vertumnus, after being spurned by the lovely Pomona, takes on various forms until he convinces her of his love. Like Vallancey, Hutchinson was quoted frequently over the next two centuries, and historians began to assume that Halloween really was simply a revamped celebration of Pomona. However, the truth was that Pomona had no festival, and that November was the dullest month in the Roman calendar, with no important holidays or festivals. But the notion that Halloween was somehow partly Roman seemed simply too delicious for most historians to give up. Take, for example, this reference from a book on Halloween dating from 1935: after discussing 'The Vigil of Samhain' (and, incidentally, referring to 'Samhain, the lord of death'), the author states: 'Our Hallowe'en is almost equally descended from the ancient Roman festival in honor of Pomona, the goddess of fruit and gardens, who was honored about the first of November.'[9] Amusingly, the next paragraph offers a compounding of errors when it is suggested that Halloween has been fused into 'a single magic celebration . . . sacred both to Samhain and Pomona'.[10]

Samhain's existence, however, is unquestionable, and some time in the mid-eighth century, Pope Gregory III moved the feast of the martyrs to 1 November, the date of Samhain, and indicated that it was henceforth to be a celebration of 'all the saints'; a hundred years later, Gregory IV ordered universal observance of the day. Was the date moved to 1 November so that the harvest could be used to feed the hordes of pilgrims flocking to Rome for the saints' celebration, as some historians have suggested? Or was it relocated in the calendar in an attempt to co-opt Samhain, which the Christianized Celts were slow to give up? A famed ninth-century Irish religious calendar, the *Martyrology of Oengus the Culdee*, offers intriguing clues: later English translations of the entry for 1 November give the day as 'stormy All-Saints' day', but the original Irish text plainly shows 'samain'.[11]

The Church provided another argument in favour of the 1 November date being chosen as a deliberate Samhain replacement when, around AD 1000, it added the celebration of All Souls' Day on 2 November. Legend has it that All Souls' Day was inaugurated in 998 by Odilon, Bishop of Cluny, after he heard of an island where a cave mouth emitted the agonized sounds of souls in torment. The official explanation given for the new festival was that it would offer the living a chance to pray for the souls of the deceased, especially those in Purgatory; however, it seems more likely that the gloomy, ghostly new celebration was added to cement the transformation of Samhain from pagan to Christian holiday. By the fourteenth century, All Souls' Day was observed throughout the western Church and had been added to all official books and calendars.

It's no coincidence, then, that the first recorded celebrations of Halloween begin to appear about this time. The *Festyvall* of 1511 says: 'We rede in olde tyme good people wolde on All Halowen daye bake brade and dele it for crysten soules',[12] suggesting that the practice of making special foods for Halloween was already long established. A *Festivall* from 1493 noted, 'Good frendes suche a daye ye shall haue all halowen daye.'[13] By the sixteenth century, there are numerous accounts in parish records of 'full contention of the ryngeres on alhallow nyght',[14] meaning that Halloween was sounded out with the raucous ringing of bells. Henry VIII tried to abolish 'ringing of bells all the night long upon Allhallow Day at night',[15] as did his daughter Elizabeth, but many parishes were so reluctant to give up the practice that their bell-ringers were repeatedly fined.

In some areas, Halloween marked the beginning of the Christmas season, and thus was the time to choose a 'Lord of Misrule' – typically a serving man in a lord's household – to oversee the merriment. One account from 1598 notes:

These Lords, beginning their rule at Allhallond Eve, continued the same till the morrow after the Feast of the Purification, commonly called Candlemas Day: in which space there were fine and subtle disguisings, masks, and mummeries.[16]

The use of Lords of Misrule was officially banned in Scotland (where they were called 'Abbots of Unreason') in 1555, and fell out of favour throughout most of England in the 1600s, partly because religious reformers considered the practice to stem from the Roman Saturnalia, also a December festival.

By 1550, Samhain had been completely absorbed into the dual festival of All Saints and All Souls, and yet the Christian celebrations retained much of the pagan character, still offering both joyful celebration and sombre contemplation of death. But there were other events happening in Europe that had become just as central to the evolution and future of Halloween.

Hans Holbein the Younger, *The Dance of Death: The Duchess*, 1523–5, woodcut.

Erhard Schoen, *Burning of a Witch*, 1533, woodcut.

In 1346, the Black Death began to rampage throughout the western hemisphere. Although it would reappear at intervals for the next 400 years, it peaked in about 1350, killing as much as 60 per cent of Europe's population. It not only left Europe reeling from the loss of human life but also changed popular culture, introducing a new obsession with images of death into the arts. The plague and the printing press were both spreading, and soon images of the *Danse Macabre* featuring gruesome skeletal figures became widely available to the surviving population. The new common obsession with depictions of skeletal Grim Reapers found a natural home in a festival once thought to be the night when the dead crossed over into the world of the living.

Following in the footsteps of the Black Death was another kind of epidemic: witch-hunts. Beginning in about 1480, tens of thousands of people – mostly women – were imprisoned, beheaded, hanged or burned alive at the stake as witches. They were sometimes accused of having killed by creating or spreading plague, and thanks to such

A postcard of 1909 warning to 'Beware of ye wiles of Satan'.

works as the *Malleus Maleficarum*, which became the manual for witch-hunters, they were commonly associated with the Devil, even to the point of accusations of sexual relations (one entire section of the *Malleus* is 'Concerning Witches who copulate with the Devil'[17]). The witch trials allowed both feudal lords and the Church to prosper by seizing the property of those charged, and solidified the image of the witch as a malicious hag with broom, cauldron and cat, three symbols of feminine housekeeping. In some trials, the victims were accused of having participated in gatherings and 'Sabbaths' held on All Hallows'. The choice of All Hallows' as a major holiday for witches and devils was no doubt coerced from the accused with a political agenda in mind: after Henry VIII ascended the throne in 1509, he sought to separate the Church of England from the Vatican, a struggle that continued with Henry's daughter, Elizabeth I. Both Henry and Elizabeth viewed All Saints' Day as a papal holiday, and both issued proclamations intended to subdue celebration of it: after Henry's ban on bell-ringing, Elizabeth extended the law to include 'the superstitious ringing of bells on Allhallowntide and at All Souls' Day, with the two nights before and after'.[18] A spectacular witch trial took place during the reign of the Protestant king James I: in 1590, dozens of Scots were accused of having attempted to prevent James from reaching his queen-to-be, Anne of Denmark, by gathering on Halloween night and then riding the sea in sieves while creating storms by tossing live cats tied to human body parts into the water. After the infamous North Berwick Witch Trials, as they were called, Halloween was forever to be firmly associated with witches, cats, cauldrons, brooms and the Devil.

The latter figure could certainly be called Halloween's most controversial icon. The Devil, that fallen angel who is the antagonist of Christianity, appears frequently in reference to Halloween and under a variety of names, including Satan, Lucifer, Beelzebub, Mephistopheles (from *Faust*) and Old Scratch. Some historians have suggested that the Devil may have originated as a way to transform pagan horned gods – including the Greeks' Pan and the Celts' Cernunnos – into a symbol of evil. The Devil first appears in relation to Halloween as the god, consort and leader of witches. For example, in 1597 a Scot named Thomas Leyis who was eventually burned as a witch was accused

> of having come upon Halloween about midnight, accompanied by his mother (since burnt) and many other sorcerers and witches, to the market and fish-cross of Aberdeen, under the conduct and guiding of the devil, present with them all in company, playing before them on his kind of instruments, when they all danced about both the said crosses and the meal market, a long pace of time ... [19]

There are numerous other accounts of witches dancing with the Devil on Halloween night, and Scottish boys were supposed to notice that their cats were tired on the day after Halloween, from carrying witches to feasts with the Devil. Many fortune-telling charms were performed in the name of the Devil, and in Aberdeenshire boys would flee a dying Halloween bonfire while exclaiming, 'The devil take the hindmost!' By the arrival of the twentieth century, the Devil had been reduced to little more than a humorous imp, usually portrayed in a red costume with horns and a tail, either appearing as a quaint paper decoration or assisting a witch on a colourful postcard. Halloween parties even featured the Devil in foods – devil's food cake and devilled eggs made frequent appearances on October menus – and later in the century, when costumes were mass-produced, devils were perpetual bestsellers.

And yet just when it seemed the Devil had been consigned to a hell of trivial merchandising, he was resurrected by late twentieth-century fundamentalist Christian groups that tagged Halloween 'The Devil's Birthday'. Christian books and websites suggested that Halloween 'is closely connected with worship of the Enemy of this world, Satan', and urged parents to keep their children from engaging in trick or treating or any other Halloween activity.[20] These groups often cite Vallancey as giving 'proof' of the day's diabolical origins, and some even go so far as to condemn church-held 'harvest parties' intended to replace Halloween activities on 31 October.

Bonfire Night

In 1605, a human devil nearly drove a stake through Halloween's heart. In the early hours of the morning of 5 November, a Catholic gentleman named Guy Fawkes (or Guido, as he'd come to call himself after a failed mission to secure Spanish support for English Catholics) was discovered beneath the House of Lords with 36 barrels of gunpowder. Although the plot had been organized largely by Robert Catesby and involved around a dozen other conspirators – all Catholics unhappy with James I's attempts at suppressing their religion – it was Fawkes who would become the man most associated with the 'Gunpowder Plot'. Fawkes, who was subjected to so much torture that he was literally unable to climb the gallows to his own execution, was hanged, drawn and quartered on 31 January 1606, but his failed attempt at assassinating the King was far from forgotten. Earlier in January, Parliament had declared 5 November 'a holiday forever in thankfulness to God for our deliverance and detestation of the Papists',[21] and Guy Fawkes Day/Eve soon became one of the British calendar's most beloved festivals.

Crispijn de Passe the Elder, *The Gunpowder Plot Conspirators, c.* 1606, engraving.

For about 40 years, Guy Fawkes and Halloween existed peacefully side by side. The *Poor Robin's Almanack* of 1677 describes 5 November thus:

> Now boys with
> Squibs and crackers play,
> And bonfires' blaze
> Turns night to day.[22]

The journal for 1629 of Bulstrode Whitelocke, then a prominent young London lawyer, describes a festive Halloween evening with revellers bedecked in finery dancing at a tavern until very late into the night.[23]

All that changed in 1647, when Parliament banned all festivals except Guy Fawkes. Because of its close proximity to All Saints' and All Souls' Days on 1 and 2 November, the celebration of Guy Fawkes Day had already acquired many of the traditions that had formerly been associated with them. Bonfires had been lit on 5 November 1605 to celebrate the King's deliverance (the eve is still often known as Bonfire Night), and that tradition would continue in some form or other to contemporary times. Young people worked weeks in advance to collect fuel for the great fires, and so house-to-house begging was involved; sometimes the children even smeared their faces with charcoal and dressed in rags, a sort of early ancestor of the twentieth-century American house-to-house begging ritual of trick or treat. Pranks that could evolve into vandalism might take place, just as they did in Irish and (later) American Halloweens. In the British town of Lewes, which is famed for the grand Guy Fawkes festivities that still take place there every year, an attempt in 1779 to limit rowdiness by banning bonfires was met with threats of burning down houses instead. The bonfires, needless to say, were allowed to continue.

Guy Fawkes Day/Night soon became the preeminent autumn celebration throughout Great Britain. Celebrations varied from parish to parish (one of the most peculiar was found in Holderness, East Yorkshire, where boys used strips of leather to beat the church pews), but typically consisted of young people begging money for fireworks and gathering fuel for bonfires as well as making an effigy of Fawkes that would be thrown onto the flames. The typical brief solicitation was to beg 'a penny for the guy', but quite often the children engaged in a longer rhyming performance, of which many variations were recorded, including this version from Worcestershire as noted down in 1892:

Burning the Pope in effigy at Temple Bar, London, on Pope Night.

Don't you remember the 5th of November
Is gunpowder treason and plot?
I don't see the reason why gunpowder treason
Should ever be forgot.
A stick and a stake, for Queen Victoria's sake,
I pray master give us a faggot;
If you don't give us one, we'll take two
The better for us and the worse for you.[24]

During this recital, the boys all thumped heavy sticks on the ground at the words 'plot', 'forgot', and 'faggot'.

Adult celebrations took place in the evening, and included lighting and supervising the bonfires, although in some towns tar barrels were lit and rolled into the nearest river. In Lewes, 'bonfire societies' also dress in costume and stage large-scale parades, still witnessed by thousands. Guy Fawkes Day also has its own foods: 'bonfire parkin' is a heavy cake, and 'bonfire toffee' is made mostly from butter and black treacle.

Guy Fawkes bonfires were popular until the nineteenth century, when a practical consideration came into play: in many areas, hill-sides had been so completely stripped of vegetation that very little fuel was available anymore. Nowadays, most British cities celebrate with a civic fireworks display and perhaps a parade.

Guy Fawkes celebrations did eventually find their way west to America with English settlers, under the title 'Pope Night'; however, American leaders in the Revolutionary War (including George Washington) were opposed to the festival, since they feared its celebration might offend the religious sensibilities of their French allies. There were still scattered celebrations reported in America until the end of the nineteenth century, though the festival had lost so much of its original meaning that the name had been degraded to 'Pork Night'.

Old Samhain and Martinmas

In 1582 came an event that would, in some areas, lead to a second night of Halloween celebration: Pope Gregory XIII signed the Gregorian calendar into effect. The old Julian calendar, which had been employed throughout Europe since 45 BC, had reckoned each year at 365.25 days, but led to an error of around three days per four centuries. This made calculating the date for Easter difficult since the spring equinox kept shifting, so the Catholic church reformed the calendar. Even though the Pope decreed the change in 1582, Martin Luther had begun the Protestant Reformation 65 years earlier (on 31 October, when he presented his 'Ninety-five Theses'), and countries that had moved largely to Protestantism were slow to accept the new calendar. In Britain, it wasn't adopted until 1752, at which point the new calendar had accrued eleven days in error.

Many inhabitants of Britain and Ireland were reluctant to adopt the new calendar, especially where their beloved festivals were concerned. In Ireland, though some inhabitants started to hold their Halloween revels on 31 October, others clung to the old calendar, meaning they now celebrated their Hallows Eve on 11 November. Yet others created two celebrations, referring to 11 November as *Oiche Shean Shamhain* ('Old Samhain Eve') and 12 November as *La Shean Shamhain* ('Old Samhain Day'). In what is now Northern Ireland, 12 November was known as 'Old Halleve', and was celebrated until the early twentieth century with dancing and fortune-telling (especially the burning of nuts).

Fortunately, there was already a festival on 11 November, and soon Martinmas began to serve as the displaced Halloween. St Martin (AD 317–397) was the patron saint of the harvest, and the date of his observance day may have been chosen to replace a great feast of Jupiter, the *epulum Iovis* (just as All Saints' Day replaced Samhain). Martinmas was celebrated around Europe and the British Isles with many rituals similar to Halloween, including the settling of debts, weather customs, feasting and merrymaking and some fortune-telling. Drinking, however, was also a major part of

Martinmas, which in some areas even came to be known as 'Martinalia'. Hiring fairs were especially popular on Martinmas, and it was also a traditional time for slaughtering livestock and laying in provisions against the coming winter. Martinmas faded considerably after cattle and pig production was industrialized and meat became plentiful throughout the year.

Bonfire Night was left as the principal autumn festival in England, but Halloween was still observed in Scotland, Ireland and Wales and on the Isle of Man. And not merely observed, but celebrated with such mystery and revelry that neither religious nor political conflicts could dampen its spirit.

2

Snap-apple Night
and November Eve:
Halloween in the British Isles

By the sixteenth century, Halloween – meaning the evening of 31 October, observed separately from All Saints' Day, All Souls' Day, Guy Fawkes Day/Bonfire Night and Martinmas – was starting to creep into both folklore and the calendar of festivals observed throughout the British Isles. In areas where Celtic influence was still strong – mainly Ireland and Scotland – the festival continued to grow in popularity. Scotland especially clung to the night's aura of romance and ghostly doings, and the earliest mentions of Halloween in poetry all emanate from Scotland. The classic Scottish ballad 'Tamlane' was first recorded in 1548, and relates the romantic and eerie story of Janet, a lass who becomes pregnant by Tamlane, a young man stolen by the fairies; Janet can rescue him only on Halloween night, provided she's able to hold onto him no matter what strange and frightening transformation the fairy queen puts the young man through. In 1584, Alexander Montgomerie penned the whimsical 'Montgomeries Answere to Polwart', which includes these famous lines:

> In the hinder end of harvest, on Allhallow even,
> When our good neighbours do ride, if I read right,
> Some buckled on a bunwand, and some on a bone
> And trotting in troops from the twilight . . . [1]

Just over two centuries later, the works of Sir Walter Scott would reveal much about the morbid imagination of the Scots.

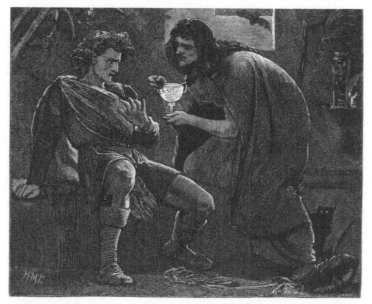

'Allison Gross', from *The English and Scottish Popular Ballads* (London, 1886).

In his *Minstrelsy of the Scottish Border* (1802–3), Scott collected ballads (including 'Tamlane'), and in the lengthy introduction he notes the superstitious nature of the Highlanders and border clans, who believed in fairies and witches, carried spell-books and thought charms had the power to cure disease.[2] Scott's own work included references to Halloween too. In his novel *The Monastery*, there are mentions of Halloween fortune-telling, encountering fetches (or the apparitions of those not yet dead), and 'second sight': 'They that are born on Hallowe'en whiles see mair than ither folk.'[3] Scott's novel *Waverley; or, 'Tis Sixty Years Since* (1814) recounts the curious legend of 'St Swithin's Chair' when one of his characters sings a song that is set on 'Hallow-mass Eve' and describes a fortune-telling custom centring on a real outcrop of rock:

He that dare sit on Saint Swithin's Chair,
When the Night-Hag wings the troubled air,

Questions three, when he speaks the spell,
He may ask, and she must tell.[4]

Another traditional Scottish ballad that probably dates from around the time of 'Tamlane' is 'Alison Gross', which once again involves a young man and a fairy queen but this time puts them in very different circumstances. At the beginning of the piece, the young man is held captive by the title character, 'the ugliest witch in the north countrie'. After she's unsuccessful at buying the young man's affections with a variety of enchanted gifts, she turns him into a snake and leaves him to 'toddle about the tree'. However, on Halloween night, the 'Seely Court', or fairies, ride by, and the queen discovers the young man; she strokes him three times, and he returns to his proper form.[5] 'Alison Gross' holds the distinction of being the only traditional Halloween tale in which a fairy undoes the work of a witch.

Thomas Hardy wrote eloquently about the fascination of bonfires in his novel *The Return of the Native* (1878); he described them as 'Druidical rites and Saxon ceremonies', and said that 'to light a fire is the instinctive and resistant act of man when, at the winter ingress, the curfew is sounded throughout Nature'.[6] Hardy was actually describing Guy Fawkes Day fires, but bonfires have been just as important to the history of Halloween. In the popular imagination, bonfires have descended in a direct line from the Celts. This excerpt from a magazine article of 1881 gives some notion of how the Celts had been romanticized:

The Druids built fires on the hill-tops in France, Britain, and Ireland, in honor of the sun. At this last festival the Druids of all the region gathered in their white robes around the stone altar or cairn on the hill-top. Here stood an emblem of the sun, and on the cairn was the sacred fire, which had been kept burning through the year. The Druids formed about the fire, and, at a signal, quenched it, while deep silence rested on the mountains and valleys. Then the new fire gleamed on the cairn, the people in the valley raised a joyous shout, and from hill-top to hill-top other fires answered the sacred flame.[7]

While this is obviously a fanciful scene, it is likely that Halloween bonfire traditions can be traced back at least to the Celtic New Year's ritual of extinguishing all fires and relighting them with an ember from a special fire kindled by the Druids.

Bonfires have an interesting history in general, beginning with the word itself, which is probably a derivation of 'bone-fire' and dates back to the burning of the bones of St John the Baptist by the Roman Emperor Julian in the fourth century AD. In AD 680, the Catholic Church attempted to abolish the practice of bonfires, and in 742 they condemned the practice of using 'needfire' (friction) to spark kindling. Obviously they were unsuccessful in their attempts, because the making of bonfires at a number of festivals, especially May Eve, Midsummer Eve and Halloween, continued throughout the centuries.

Bonfires at Halloween once served an actual purpose by getting rid of the refuse left over from the harvest, but, as previously mentioned, eventually the practice came to involve begging for firewood, mainly on the part of children. In Scotland, the fires were called *samhnag*, and could be seen on every hilltop on Halloween night. One of the most famous descriptions of a Scottish Halloween bonfire comes from the Englishman Thomas Pennant, who kept extensive journals of his travels and recorded this scene in 1772:

Hallow eve is also kept sacred: as soon as it is dark, a person sets fire to a bush of broom fastened round a pole; and, attended with a crowd, runs round the village. He then flings it down, keeps great quantity of combustible matters in it, and makes a great bonfire. A whole tract is thus illuminated at the same time, and makes a fine appearance.[8]

Occasionally, Halloween bonfires were thought to serve specific purposes. In Northern England, bonfires were lit on All

Souls' Eve (rather than Halloween) to light the way for souls out of Purgatory. These fires were sometimes called 'tindles' or 'teanloes', and Halloween was even referred to as 'Teanlay' in this district in honour of the bonfires. Another fire custom invoking that realm between Heaven and Hell was set in a Lancashire field actually named Purgatory Field; men assembled there at midnight on Halloween and tossed forkfuls of burning straw into the air while praying for souls in Purgatory. In an interview conducted in 1944, an Irish native discussed All Souls' Eve in terms of Purgatory:

> The night of the 1st–2nd November is known as *oiche Feil na Marg* – 'All Souls' Eve'. It is believed that the dead whose souls are in Purgatory are permitted to return to the ancestral home on that night. In most houses the door is left on the latch [unlocked], a good fire is kept burning all night . . . the members of the household say the family rosary and go early to bed . . . in order to leave the departed souls in undisturbed possession of the fireside.[9]

In some areas, fires were lit to protect against witches and malicious fairies. In Scotland, boys might beg for firewood in order to 'burn the witches', who might also be burned in effigy (Queen Victoria witnessed this practice during her 1869 visit to Balmoral Castle). In Lancashire, witches were thought to assemble on Halloween in the Forest of Pendle at a ruined farmhouse called the Malkin Tower. Rather than creating bonfires, fearful residents practiced 'leeting' or 'lating' the witches:

> It was believed that if a lighted candle were carried about the fells or hills from eleven to twelve o'clock at night, and burned all that time steadily, it had so far triumphed over the evil power of the witches, who as they passed to the Malkin Tower, would employ their utmost efforts to extinguish the light, and the person whom it represented might safely defy their malice during the season; but if, by any accident the candle went out,

it was an omen of evil to the luckless wight for whom the experiment was made.[10]

The province of Moray was said to hold 'a solemnity for the safe in-gathering of the produce of the fields' by lighting bonfires.[11] From Perthshire comes this eyewitness account of a spectacular fire tradition:

> On the evening of the 31st of October . . . one remarkable ceremony is observed. Heath, broom, and dressings of flax, are tied upon a pole. This faggot is then kindled. One takes it upon his shoulders; and, running, bears it round the village. A crowd attend. When the first faggot is burnt out, a second is bound to the pole, and kindled in the same manner as before. Numbers of these blazing faggots are often carried about together, and when the night happens to be dark, they form a splendid illumination. This is Halloween, and is a night of great festivity.[12]

The practice of bonfires began to die out in Britain by the end of the nineteenth century, in part because (as noted earlier) there was simply nothing left to burn, but also because of the dangers posed by bonfires to spectators – and by spectators to other spectators. James Napier, writing in 1879 about a Hallow-een spent watching boys build bonfires around Loch Tay in Scotland, noted:

> I was told by old men that at the beginning of this century men as well as boys took part in getting up the bonfires, and that, when the fire was ablaze, all joined hands and danced round the fire, and made a great noise; but that, as these gatherings generally ended in drunkenness and rough and dangerous fun, the ministers set their faces against the observance, and were seconded in their efforts by the more intelligent and well-behaved in the community; and so the practice was discontin-ued by adults and relegated to school boys.[13]

Robert Burns.

While the Halloween bonfire may have been popular, it was soon rivalled and bested by the popularity of Halloween fortune-telling rituals, and certainly no bard captured the spirit of the Scottish Halloween prophecy customs better than Robert Burns. Burns, who is sometimes referred to as 'Scotland's Favourite Son', would none the less become most well-known for penning the poem 'Auld Lang Syne', which has become something of an anthem for another holiday, New Year's Eve (or the Scottish New Year celebration Hogmanay). However, it's Burns's poem 'Hallowe'en' of 1785 that provides a far more revealing look at the traditional festival. In 252 lines, Burns describes some of the

legendary background of the holiday ('Upon that night, when
fairies light'), the favoured foods ('butter'd so'ns' – sowens is similar
to oatmeal) and, especially, the games and fortune-telling rituals.[14]

Whom Will I Marry? Halloween Fortune-telling

It's impossible to pinpoint exactly when fortune-telling games
became an integral part of Halloween festivities; most later accounts
of them simply refer back to the Burns poem, which suggests that
fortune-telling rituals were already well-established and linked to
Halloween. John Gay's 'mock pastoral' poetic work *The Shepherd's
Week* of 1714 includes some of the same fortune-telling methods,
especially the burning of nuts,[15] but makes no mention of Halloween, although it mentions other festivals, such as May Day. Indeed,
many of the fortune-telling methods later associated with Halloween have earlier connections to other celebrations, including Midsummer's Eve, St Agnes' Eve, Christmas and New Years'. It seems
likely that many of these rituals migrated to Scottish Halloween
some time in the eighteenth century, since the day's history lent
itself well to these slightly pagan practices.

The vast majority of these fortune-telling games were dedicated to learning the nature of one's future spouse – either by name,
character or profession – since marriage was probably the most
important event in the life of a rural, pre-industrial young person.
These rituals, so indelibly described by Burns and carried down all
the way to the early twentieth century, undoubtedly left a romantic
mark on Halloween forever.

In the Burns poem, the 'merry, friendly, countra folk' begin
the evening by venturing into the kale field to pull stalks. This is
possibly the most popular of the eighteenth- and nineteenth-
century fortune-telling games, and was performed in Ireland with
cabbages. There are numerous variations of this ritual – in some
the fortune-seeker must enter the field backwards or blindfolded
– but all involve examining the stalk to determine the nature of
one's future spouse. In the Burns poem, both the shape of the

stalk – 'muckle anes an' straught anes' – and the taste – 'sweet or sour' – will reveal the beloved's character. The kale stalk might also have been nailed up over the main doorway in the belief that the first young person to enter beneath would be the future spouse (or would at least bear the initials of said spouse). This activity was so popular that it was frequently referred to simply as 'kaling'.

Next up in the Burns poem is the bawdy custom of young ladies pulling 'corn' (in fact, oats); three stalks are pulled, and if the third should lack the grain at the top, the girl will not enter into marriage as a virgin. Burns has particular fun with this stanza, suggesting that Nelly loses her 'tap-pickle' to Rob while practicing this very custom.

The next four stanzas are devoted to burning nuts. Here's how Gay described the practice in the 'Thursday' section of *The Shepherd's Week*:

> Two hazel-nuts I threw into the flame
> And to each nut I gave a sweet-heart's name.[16]

The nut that blazed brightest and longest indicated the truest lover. In 'Hallowe'en', however, the two nuts are named for the lovers, and depending on whether they burn together to ash or jump away from each other, so will the relationship progress.

Next, Burns introduces Merran, who retires to the lime-kiln (a large brick structure used for producing quicklime and a common fixture on eighteenth-century farms) for a custom involving blue yarn. In the classic version of this fortune-telling stunt, the girl threw her clew (or ball) into the kiln and would soon feel something tugging on the yarn, at which point she cried out, 'Who holds?' She would then hear the name of her future husband, which – needless to say – was likely uttered by the hidden boy himself. This particular fortune-telling method was especially subject to pranking, as in this example quoted by John Gregorson Campbell in *Witchcraft and Second Sight in the Highlands and Islands of Scotland*:

There is a story of a tailor having hid himself in anticipation of this mode of divination being resorted to, and when the ball was thrown he caught it and gave the thread a tug. In answer to the question 'who is this at the end of my little rope?' he said, 'I am the devil'... and the woman to whom this frightful answer was given never tried divination again.[17]

Burns briefly mentions a method that was popular even into the twentieth century in which a curious young lady would stand before a mirror on Halloween night with an apple and, after either eating it or slicing it into sections, would see the face of her beloved reflected in the glass. In her collection of Irish legends, Lady Jane Wilde recounts this frightening result from someone who performed this ritual on Halloween night:

A lady narrates that on the 1st of November her servant rushed into the room and fainted on the floor. On recovering, she said that she had played a trick that night in the name of the devil before the looking-glass; but what she had seen she dared not speak of, though the remembrance of it would never leave her brain, and she knew the shock would kill her. They tried to laugh her out of her fears, but the next night she was found quite dead, with her features horribly contorted, lying on the floor before the looking-glass, which was shivered to pieces.[18]

In 'Hallowe'en', Grannie warns little Jenny that 'Nae doubt but ye may get a *sight*!' and recounts a frightful story from her own youth involving the sowing of hemp seed. In this divination, the fortune-seeker went into a hemp field, sowed seed behind him or her, and recited a small rhyme, which Burns gives as:

Hemp seed I saw thee,
Hemp seed I saw thee;
And him (or her) that is to be my true-love,
Come after me and pou thee.[19]

The Devil waits behind the Halloween mirror: 'All Hallows Eve' by Mme
Boulanger, engraved by A. H. Putchie.

Burns offers an amusing twist to this ritual, when the seeker, a bold
young man named Jamie Fleck, is startled by the sudden appearance
of a pig.

Many of these classic Halloween divinations involved belief
in the 'wraith' or 'fetch', which was essentially the spirit of someone
not yet dead. Invisible spirits attached to each person, wraiths could

All Hallowe'en Greetings

Our future in the present we still sow,
And ever anxious, sometimes seek to know
Events before they happen—and we fall,
And thus provide a hearty laugh to all
On Hallowe'en.

Burns's Jamie Fleck meets the sow in this postcard.

occasionally separate themselves and become visible to others. Scottish folklore expert James Napier, when discussing the wraith, mentions the biblical story of Peter knocking on the door of a house while he was in prison, and also the classic Scottish song 'Auld Robin Gray', in which a woman meeting her old sweetheart exclaims, 'I thought it was his wraith'.[20] In Ireland, this supernatural double was called a fetch, and was believed to foretell good tidings if seen in the morning, but death if glimpsed in the afternoon or evening. The fetch was usually believed to represent someone suffering from a prolonged illness, but on Halloween it appeared as a prophecy of marriage. In his article 'Hallowe'en: A Three-fold Chronicle' of 1886, William Sharp describes a magical encounter told to him by a resident of Perthshire: at fourteen, a young lady named Madge Falconer fell in love with her seventeen-year-old neighbour Ralph Morgan. Before they were both old enough to wed, however, Ralph moved to India, and Madge didn't see him for nearly seven years. On the Halloween, just before her twenty-first birthday, she tried the looking-glass prognostication, and beheld not Ralph but an older man with a particular scar. She moved to India shortly thereafter, met again with Ralph, but soon realized she was no longer in love with him. Not long after she met a man named Major Colville and recognized his as the face she'd seen on Halloween, complete with the scar he had taken during a battle with Sikhs. She and Colville were soon married.[21]

One of the most fearsome examples of a custom involving a wraith is recounted in the Burns work when Meg heads to the barn 'To *win three wechts o' naething*.' In this fortune-telling ritual, the seeker went to a barn and opened both doors (preferably removing them from their hinges, lest they close on their own and seal the victim in with a menacing spirit), took down the wecht, or the instrument used in winnowing corn, and pantomimed the act of separating corn from chaff three times. At the completion of this task, a spectre bearing the appearance of one's future intended would pass through the barn. The fortune-seeker must perform all of this after calling on the Devil, which no doubt gave Halloween a particularly sinister air.

Stacks of barley figured into a fortune-telling method referred to as 'fadomin' da skroo': the fortune-seeker went blindfolded three times around a stack of barley (some variants of this tradition specify that it must be done 'widdershins', meaning 'against the sun' or anticlockwise), and at the end of the last turn would embrace the future beloved. In the Burns poem, young Will attempts this, but is unaware that he actually walked three times around a stack of timber by mistake; he is startled when he comes face-to-face with a rotted piece of oak that he mistakes for an aged woman.

Many of the now obsolete fortune-telling rituals involved water, but perhaps none was as popular as 'the dipping of the sark sleeve'. Burns says this must be performed 'whare three lairds' lands meet at a burn', and at that point a young woman would dip her sleeve into the water, then return home to set the shirt to dry by the hearth-fire. The lass would then retire to bed, and during the night would see her intended enter the room and turn the shirt, so that the other side would dry as well. Of course Burns once again shows Halloween as a night of playful scares when his lady is startled by a sound (which could be either the Devil or a bird) and plunges into the water.

A real account of late eighteenth-century sleeve-dipping illustrates, however, that Halloween fortune-telling wasn't always considered an innocent game. Records from Eastwood relate the confession of a woman who had used charms at Halloween and who said that,

> at the instigation of an old woman from Ireland, she brought in a pint of water from a well which brides and burials pass over, and dipt her shirt into it, and hung it before the fire; that she either dreamed, or else there came something and turned about the chair on which her shirt was, but she could not well see what it was. Her sentence was a rebuke before the congregation.[22]

Another ritual involving water was referred to as the luggie bowls. 'Luggies' are small bowls with handles ('lugs'). In this tradition, three of them would be filled with different substances and arrayed before a blindfolded fortune-seeker, whose future was foretold by whether he touched the dish of clean water (marriage to a virgin), dirty water (marriage to a widow) or nothing (no marriage would occur). The luggie bowls are one of the most common of all Halloween games, and there are dozens of variants; in some, the bowls hold not water but objects (a thimble, for example, symbolizes spinsterhood). The number of bowls might be as high as six, or the game might be played without using bowls at all. A nineteenth-century version instructed that three tin cups partially full of water should be placed on the small ends of three funnels, which would be set up in a line on the floor. The young ladies should then take turns at leaping over each of these constructions, with the number of cups knocked over dictating the time until marriage would take place (in the case of an unlucky miss who caught her skirts on all three cups, she would remain single).

The luggie bowls figure prominently in James Joyce's poignant Halloween story 'Clay'. Published in 1914, 'Clay' describes an urban Irish Halloween party, and centres on the tragedy of Maria, an unmarried woman who first touches the dish of clay (an early death), and then the prayer-book (a life devoted to God, not a husband). In Burns's poem, a similar twist is played for humour: when Uncle

John touches the empty dish three times in a row, signifying a life as a single man, he's so infuriated that he hurls the three bowls into the fire.

Fortune-telling games were also being played in Ireland during the eighteenth- and nineteenth-centuries, but door-to-door begging figured even more prominently. Prognostication involving cabbage-pulling, nut-burning, sowing of hemp seed, lime kilns and dipping the sleeve in water are all recorded, but so is a begging ritual practiced in honor of St Columba, a sixth-century missionary who converted many Irish and Scottish pagans. Columba – or 'Colum Kill', as he came to be known by the 1700s – was invoked by Irish peasants who went door to door demanding money to buy 'fatted calves and black sheep' for a feast in the saint's name.

Another Irish Halloween costuming ritual was presented by the 'Strawboys', a group of young men dressed in distinctive suits made of white straw and tall, conical hats, who engaged in wild pranking and petty vandalism (especially stealing food) directed mainly at families who kept their daughters from the company of boys. The Strawboys also appeared at weddings, where they would demand a dance with the bride, and this tradition has continued into modern times. Some Irish wedding planners, in fact, offer an appearance by the Strawboys as an optional paid extra.

In Northern Ireland, door-to-door Halloween rhyming occurs for several weeks prior to the actual night of Halloween. Young people may beg at the same houses several times, and may receive money, which they use to buy fireworks. The fireworks are likewise set off throughout this period, while 31 October is reserved for bonfires and family dinners.

A similar, though even stranger, tradition is recorded in the Shetland Islands off the coast of Scotland. There, a group of young men called the Grülacks, dressed in exotic costumes ornamented with coloured ribbons, tall hats and veils, paid surprise visits to houses on Halloween, demanding food and liquor. Their arrival was announced by firing a shot over the house, and the homeowner had to fire a welcoming round before they would enter. They would file into the kitchen, led by a character called 'the skuddler',

Testing fate with the three luggie bowls.

On Hallowe'en.
By pumpkin's light, This witch
Will help you choose aright.

and bang long sticks on the floor until they were offered food; they also were usually accompanied by a fiddler, and would present some sort of performance before leaving. Like the Strawboys, the Grülacks were also a popular fixture at weddings, and by the twentieth century they were associated almost exclusively with weddings and Christmas.

Fairies, Pookas and Witches

Both the Scottish and the Irish had a considerable amount of folklore centred on fairies, or *sidh*, and Halloween appears frequently in this lore. The fact that belief in fairies was found primarily among the descendants of the Celts lends credence to the theory that the fairies are the old gods reduced to small, supernatural imps by Christianity; however, in some fairy stories, the fairies also seem to be connected to the spirits of the dead. Lady Wilde, for instance, recorded a traditional Irish story called 'November Eve' in which a fisherman named Hugh King stays out too late on Halloween, and encounters a large band of merrymakers who tell him they are bound for a fair. Hugh accompanies them, meets Finvarra, the king of the fairies, and then is pulled into a dance by the spirit of a dead woman. Hugh survives the dreadful night, but in the morning realizes that the fairies mocked and taunted him because he ignored warnings to stay inside on Halloween night.

The fairies were thought to live within the grassy hillocks that dotted the landscapes of Ireland and Scotland, and only on Halloween might these fairy raths open to mortals. One Scottish belief had it that a mortal who walked nine times in an anticlockwise direction around one of the *sidh*-mounds on Halloween night would be admitted to the fairy realm, where he would experience the pleasures of that world; however, he would be unable to return to his mortal existence, and would become forever a *shi ich*, or 'man of peace'. Fairies might also choose to leave their barrows and visit mortals: a passage from a fifteenth-century historical text called *The Book of Fermoy* relates the story of Fingen mac Luchta, King of Munster in the third century, who was visited on Samhain night by Bacht, a fairy woman, who told him of 50 wonders.

Usually the fairies were not so kindly disposed towards humans. In *The Golden Bough* (1922), Sir James Frazer relates a Scottish yarn of two young men who, on Halloween night, encountered a brightly lit house full of jigging merrymakers; one of the young men immediately entered and joined in the fun, but the other suspected that the 'house' might actually be a fairy knoll. This young man took the precaution of placing a needle in the doorway before entering, and thus disarmed the power of the fairies and escaped safely. His companion, however, was trapped in the fairy rath for a year, and when Halloween came around again he was found still dancing before he collapsed into a pile of bones.

In Northern Ireland, families were cautious about allowing children out on Halloween night because of fairies well into the early twentieth century. If a child set foot on ben-weed on Halloween night, he or she was certain to be carried off by the 'little people'. For protection, parents might rub a mixture of dry oatmeal and salt into the hair of any child venturing out on Halloween night. Babies were also at risk, since fairies might steal the infant and replace it with a 'stock', or fairy child. The stock sometimes had the appearance of a tiny, old, bearded man who never aged; or the baby might appear normal, but would soon sicken and die. A baby could be protected on Halloween night by placing something made of iron in or over its crib. A fairy child might be detected by boiling eggshells in its presence; this would cause the tot to utter an adult exclamation and thus give away its true nature.

The mischievous 'good people' (this euphemism was spoken in order to not risk offending the fairies) were also fond of carrying off attractive adult humans, who could usually only be rescued on Halloween. The ballad of Tamlane is the classic example of this, but Sir Walter Scott also records (in his introduction to 'Tamlane') the tale of a Lothian farmer whose wife was stolen by fairies, and who appeared to him repeatedly for a year after her kidnapping, telling him how to rescue her come Halloween night. However, when the fateful evening arrived, the farmer was so frightened by the 'wild unearthly sound' of the fairy troupe that he was paralysed, and could only stand helplessly listening to the mournful cries of his wife as she passed him by one last time before being lost forever.

Brave humans might use the Halloween power of fairies for their own ends. In the Irish legend of 'Guleesh Na Guss Dhu', an abused young man named Guleesh joins the fairies on Halloween night on a magical ride to France, where the fairies beg Guleesh's help in kidnapping a beautiful princess before her wedding. Guleesh agrees, but first demands to be taken to Rome, where the fairies assist him in forcing the Pope to reinstate Guleesh's parish priest. In France, Guleesh and the fairies successfully make off with the girl and return to Ireland, but Guleesh decides to keep the princess for himself. The fairies curse the princess, removing her power of

Fairies emerge from their barrow on Halloween night in this postcard of 1912.

speech, but on the following Halloween, Guleesh overhears some of the fairies describing a cure for the princess's affliction, and is thus able to banish the curse. He and the princess are then married.

One of the most curious Scottish Halloween creatures was found on Lewis, an island in the Outer Hebrides. On Halloween night, families assembled at the church of St Mulway, where each provided a bag of malt that was brewed into ale. One man was then chosen to wade into the sea with a cup of this ale, at which point he recited: 'Shony, I give you this cup of ale, hoping that you'll be so kind as to send us plenty of sea-ware [seaweed], for enriching our ground the ensuing year.'[23] After hurling the ale into the sea, the man waded back to shore and the entire assemblage returned to the church, where they spent a few solemn moments in contemplation of a candle. When the candle was extinguished, the remainder of the night was devoted to drinking the ale and dancing in the fields. The origin of the name 'Shony' has been lost in history, although it may be derived from 'Seonaidh', the Scottish Gaelic version of 'Johnny', suggesting that this ritual is actually honouring one of the Christian saints named John.

Some of the grimmest of Halloween beliefs were found among the Welsh, and the Welsh continued to observe the day for longer than their English neighbours. A book of 1849 notes the Welsh fondness for festivals and offers some insight into why Halloween was more beloved by members of the working class:

> Old festival days, with their games and merriment, superstitions and legends, which have gone or are fast going into forgetful-ness in England, are still important and still observed in Wales. All-Hallows' Eve, so famous in Scottish and Irish story, is here no less celebrated, and its customs no less kept. It is the people of the locality and the soil, who are not worn into the smooth-ness of general society by intercourse with large towns, that devote themselves to these observances; and thus the labourers and the old women of the village are they particularly who expect and keep Hollantide.[24]

Halloween's name in Wales was *Nos Calan Gaeaf*, which meant 'night of the winter calends', although the Welsh also considered Halloween the most unearthly of the *Teir Nos Ysbrydion*, or 'Three Spirit Nights' (the other two were May Eve and Midsummer's Eve). On those three nights, the spirits of those who had drowned might surface once again, riding white horses atop the waves. A typical nineteenth-century Welsh Halloween party might include such ordinary diversions as bobbing for apples, snap-apple and fortune-telling games, such as burning nuts on the hearth – but the way the nuts blazed determined whether those who had tossed them into the flames would still be alive next Halloween, not whom they were likely to marry. The Welsh were believers in the custom of the church porch, in which those who were brave enough to stand by the church windows at midnight on Halloween might hear a sermon delivered by Satan in which he would reveal the names of all those from the parish who would die during the coming year; of course, the listener ran the risk of hearing his or her own name spoken. In another version of this belief, the curious were instructed to hide in the churchyard on Halloween night; at midnight they would witness a procession of all those in the parish who would die in the coming year, although any member of the procession who abruptly turned back indicated someone who would suffer a serious illness but recover. Welsh women also gathered in churches on Halloween, believing they could read fates there from flickering candle flames.

The Welsh called fairies *tylweth teg*, and had many stories about supernatural occurrences on Halloween. One begins with a hiring fair on Halloween, when a kindly older couple hire a lovely young serving girl to work for them. The girl disappears after a time, and a year later the wife is called one night to serve as midwife. She is taken to a fairy hillock, where she sees the most beautiful room she has ever visited; however, upon accidentally rubbing a fairy potion into one eye, she realizes the new mother is her former servant girl, and the room is actually little more than a cave. The serving girl's fairy husband puts the wife's anointed eye out with a stick.

Welsh belief in witches and other superstitions also ran strong. They believed that as long as consecrated bells rang they were protected from witches on Halloween; *bwyd cennad y meirw* was food left out for the dead on Halloween; wind blowing over the feet of corpses on Halloween would create a sighing sound that predicted death to any who heard it; one could also listen to the wind in a crossroads on Halloween night to receive omens of the coming year; hearing crows around a house on Halloween meant that someone in the house would soon die; and at Maes-Y-Felin Field anyone who went to the ancient ruins known as the 'Druidical stones' and whispered a wish to them would find that wish coming true during the following year.

The Welsh word *pwca* (goblin) led to the word 'pooka' or 'puca', a malicious fairy or demonic creature that appeared in folklore from all over the British Isles. The pooka was a shape-shifter who was seen on Halloween night in the form of a horse; if it was a 'water-horse' that arose from a loch or other body of water, it would make a splendid steed if captured, but could also rip apart those who approached it. In Scotland, they told the story of the *each-uisg*, or water-horse, that lived in Loch Dorch; one Halloween, a foolish young girl decided to try the Halloween fortune-telling custom of dipping her sleeve in water, and vanished forever, leaving behind only her screams in the night and shreds of clothing found next morning near a hoof-print. The name 'pooka' also led to 'Puck', who of course featured as the lead mischievous sprite in Shakespeare's *A Midsummer Night's Dream*.

The Welsh had their own Halloween bonfire ritual as well. Called *coel coeth*, the literal translation of which means 'an omen of danger', the bonfire was built on Halloween by a family on a prominence near their house. Each family member made a mark on a white stone which was then thrown into the fire; on the following morning, any stone that couldn't be found foretold the death of its owner within the year. Young people also cast nuts into the bonfire, and when the nuts burst or shot out, they fled in terror of 'the goblin black-tailed sow' (the *Hwch du gwta*) who was thought to be abroad on Halloween.

The Welsh weren't all about death and goblins, however; they also believed in the Halloween fetch who might reveal the identity of a future spouse. In one tradition, young women assembled before midnight around a dining table, and turned all the silverware upside-down; at midnight, they might see their intended enter to turn everything to rights again. One Welsh woman who recounted this custom added an interesting twist to the lore of the fetch: she did indeed claim to have witnessed the apparition of a man entering to turn the silverware, but none of the other three women with her saw a thing. A short time later, she met the man in person for the first time, and they were soon married.

Foods, Fairs and Other British Traditions

Halloween had a number of its own food traditions, many of which have continued to the present day. Certainly no food is more identified with Halloween in all of its various times and locations than the apple. The association of the apple and Halloween likely dates back to the Celts; although we have no specific connections drawn between Samhain and apples, apples certainly abound in every other part of Celtic mythology. The mythic trees of the divine island Elysium grew three fruits: apples, acorns and nuts. In the tragic story of star-crossed lovers Ailinn and Baile, an apple tree grew from Ailinn's grave and the apples bore the face of her beloved Baile. The chief god (and father of hero Angus Og) the Dagda lived in a kingdom where there were always apple trees in fruit, to say nothing of a neverending supply of ale. In the epic 'Voyages of Maildun', the eponymous hero feeds his starving crew at one point when he encounters an island with a magical apple tree whose fruits supply the sailors for 40 days and nights. There has even been some speculation that the Celts brought apple-growing with them when they first came to the British Isles.

Given that apples ripen in October, and that Samhain was held at the end of that month, it seems likely that apples would have been plentiful at Celtic Samhain feasts. Later Halloween celebrations weren't content to use the apple only as a menu item, but also employed it in games, fortune-telling and decoration. In some areas of Ireland, 1 November was once called *La Mas Ubhal* – 'the day of the apple' – and in parts of the British Isles Halloween is still celebrated with a drink made of apples and ale called 'lamb's wool', a corruption of the name. One particularly piquant description of producing lamb's wool states that on Halloween, the apple was roasted on a string until it dropped off into a bowl of spiced ale set beneath it.

A journal article on Halloween written in 1844 notes that 'The custom of bobbing for apples on All Hallow E'en, and on All Saints Day, which was formerly common over all England . . . is still practised in some parts of Ireland . . .'.[25] This suggests that bobbing (or ducking) for apples had fallen out of favour in most areas of England by then. Robert Burns makes no mention of the custom in his classic work but a poem of 1792 by a contemporary, Janet Little, mentions snap-apple, a risky game in which an apple was placed on one end of a suspended stick and a lit candle at the other; the stick was then spun, and the object was to retrieve a mouthful of apple instead of hot wax. This game was so popular that Halloween became known as 'Snap-apple Night' in some areas (or, in Wales, 'Snotching Night', from the act of snatching the apple). Likewise, the name 'Nutcrack Night' – derived from burning nuts on the hearth to tell fortunes – was sometimes used in Northern England.

Bobbing for apples had been a popular pastime in Britain for at least 400 years, with the fourteenth-century illuminated manuscript *The Luttrell Psalter* showing a lord's servants engaged in the game, but by the nineteenth century it may have been confined to Ireland and just a few areas of England. In his *Observations on Popular Antiquities* (1810), John Brand's entry on Halloween begins with apples, although he suggests that bobbing is limited to only the north of England:

> It is customary on this Night for young People in the North to *dive* for apples, catch at them when stuck on to one End of a Kind of hanging beam, at the other Extremity of which is fixed a lighted Candle, and that with their Mouths only, having their Hands tied behind their Backs; and many other Fooleries.[26]

In 1833, London painter Daniel Maclise created a small stir in the art world with his painting *Snap-apple Night*, which had been inspired by a trip to Ireland in 1832 and a visit to a Halloween party held by an esteemed local priest, Father Mathew Horgan. In the painting, party guests are shown both playing snap-apple and bobbing for apples.

Bobbing for apples might function as both a party game and a fortune-telling ritual. The game offered alternatives such as spearing

Bobbing for apples.

an apple with a fork dropped from above, and retrieving an apple with a small extra prize, such as a coin, inserted into it. The element of augury, however, could be added simply by carving initials into the apples and seeing whose apple each player could successfully retrieve, or by placing a bit of a retrieved apple under the pillow that night to invite prophetic dreams.

Burns may not have rhymed about bobbing for apples, but he did mention the fortune-telling ritual of eating an apple before a mirror at midnight on Halloween, which went on to be one of the most oft-reported and popular of the Halloween fortune-telling stunts. There were dozens of variants on this ritual: in some the lass was required to brush her hair as she ate the apple, while in others it was necessary to slice the apple into nine sections, with the future intended appearing to receive the final slice.

Parts of apples were used in a number of fortune-telling customs. The skin of the apple might be pared, and then flung over the left shoulder as this rhyme (adapted from Gay's *The Shepherd's Week*) was recited:

> I pare this pippin round and round again,
> My sweetheart's name to flourish on the plain;
> I fling the unbroken paring o'er my head,
> My sweetheart's letter on the ground is read.[27]

The apple paring was then examined to find the shape of an initial which would indicate the name of one's future spouse.

Apple seeds were also put to use. The apple was cut open, and the number of visible seeds indicated the future (two meant early marriage, three augured wealth, and so on). Seeds might be used on a hearth in place of nuts, or might be named and stuck to the skin of the face or hands. The first to fall might indicate the failed suitor, or the number of seeds remaining after a clap might indicate the number of years until marriage.

An article of 1822 recounting an Englishman's visit to an Irish Halloween party notes that two young women entertained themselves by naming a pair of apples after a local lord and lady, then roasting them on the fire to laugh at the way they furiously sputtered and foamed.

Nuts were also revered by the Celts, and have been another staple of late harvest Halloween celebrations ever since. The custom of burning nuts on Halloween night to find the identity of one's future spouse or the temperament of the relationship was practised equally in Ireland, Scotland, the northern parts of England and America, at least until ovens replaced open hearths. Chestnuts, walnuts and hazelnuts were those most often used, and one custom involved combining a walnut, a hazelnut and a nutmeg with some butter and sugar into small pills, which were taken just before bedtime on Halloween night to bring prophetic dreams. Walnut shells were used in a number of fortune-telling rituals: small objects might be placed inside shells that were then tied together, and the couple that could match two objects were destined for marriage; or small boats might be created from shells that were then filled with lighted candles and placed into a tub, their subsequent movements to and away from other 'boats' indicating future relationships.

Nuts also provided Halloween games: they could be hidden around a room to create a treasure hunt. Small prizes were also sometimes hidden in sealed walnut shells.

Cabbage and/or kale (or, in Wales especially, leeks) was another popular Halloween food, used in fortune-telling, pranking and a number of Halloween-specific dishes. The most common fortune-telling custom was that described by Burns, in which young people pulled cabbages on Halloween, then examined and tasted the stalk to glean insight into future mates.

Mischievous boys found an almost endless number of uses for cabbage in Halloween pranking. Cabbages made convenient missiles, and might be pulled and thrown at the doors of a prankster's enemy. In one Scottish practice called 'Burning the Reekie Mehr', the stalk of the cabbage was hollowed out and filled instead with tow, which produced long flames when lit and blown (preferably through key holes). There were even stories of pranksters tying strings to cabbages in a field to give passers-by the illusion that the cabbages were moving.

Cabbage is one of the three main ingredients in colcannon, a food so popular at Halloween that 31 October was known as 'Colcannon Night' in some areas of Ireland and Scotland. Colcannon consists of cabbage, potatoes and onions mashed together, and is sometimes served with a ring or other tokens of prediction hidden inside.

Grains were also harvested around Halloween, and Burns noted the popularity of oats and barley in Halloween fortune-telling customs. The grain harvest was often celebrated by using parts of the corn to create a small doll-like figure called the corn dolly, or *cailleach*. This figure was hung in the kitchen and left there until Christmas, and was sometimes named differently (as a young maid or an old woman) depending on whether it was cut before or after Halloween.

Halloween had a variety of special cakes and baked goods, most of which also served in fortune-telling customs. The 'fortune cake' could be any cake with small tokens that represented future endeavours baked inside. Receiving a slice of cake with a coin in it, for example, foretold wealth, while a ring represented marriage and a thimble, spinsterhood. The 'dumb cake' was made from a simple dough that a group of girls prepared together in silence; at the end of baking, the girls' future husbands would supposedly appear to take a piece. In Ireland, a special bread known as 'barm brack' remains a Halloween tradition; made from strong black tea and various dried fruits, barm brack is usually baked with fortune-telling pieces inside.

In Ireland, boxty has long been a familiar Halloween food item. A pancake made from potatoes and flour, boxty (from the Irish *bachstai*, meaning 'poor house bread'), was popular on both Halloween and Boxing Day menus. Another popular Irish Halloween food based on potatoes was champ, in which potatoes were mashed with milk, butter and spring onions, with fortune-telling tokens usually hidden inside. Stampy was a sweet potato cake served on Halloween, made with potatoes, sugar, cream and caraway seeds.

But perhaps no food item was as important as the soul-cake. 'Souling' or 'soul-caking' once took place throughout the British Isles, and (since it was reported in the 1511 edition of *Festyvall*) is one of the earliest reported Halloween activities. Distribution of soul-cakes was reported as late as the beginning of the twentieth century in some areas (especially Derbyshire, Lancashire, Shropshire and Cheshire), and typically took place late on 1 November (All Souls' Eve). Souling mostly involved children, although sometimes adults took part as well. One description from 1880 includes a version of a traditional souling rhyme:

> The children go round to the houses early and late on All Saints' day, not on All Souls' day, and sing monotonously a doggerel; the lines vary a little with the groups of children, three to six in a group. The most complete version I can give you is as follows:
>
> > Soul! soul! a soul-cake;
> > Good mistress, gi' us a soul-cake,
> > One for Peter, one for Paul
> > And one for them as made us all.
> > An apple or a cherry
> > Or anything else to make us merry.
> > Oh! good mistress, to the cellar
> > And fetch us a pail of water.
> > It is a good fame
> > To get a good name.[28]

In some areas, children engaged in souling in the morning, while servants or farm workers went from house to house in the evening, begging food and beer. The adults sometimes accompanied themselves with small musical instruments (such as a concertina), and in both cases the groups may have blackened their faces and/or carried with them a 'hobby horse'. The hobby horse – sometimes referred to as 'dobby horse' or 'Old Hob' – was frequently a macabre creation, consisting of a real horse's skull mounted atop a staff and carried by a man draped in a sheet or skin. Hobby horses were usually part of Christmas mumming plays, in which a troupe of adult actors went from house to house on Christmas Eve or Day and presented a variant of the old play *St George and the Turk*, but they also made an appearance at Halloween.

The ritual of souling included, of course, both those who were begging and the homeowners who handed out food, drink and coins; however, the most important item was the 'soul cake' (known in some areas as 'saumas cakes' or 'saumas loaves'). These were small round seedcakes made with spices and with currants on top, and were themselves considered good luck. They were often kept instead of eaten. Certain homeowners had soul cakes that they had kept for years; one woman in Whitby was said in 1817 to have a soul cake that was a century old.

The Isle of Man had its own particular and peculiar customs. The Manx name for Halloween was 'Hollantide' or 'hop-tu-naa' (pronounced 'hop-chew-nay'), which may have been derived from the Scottish name for New Year's, Hogmanay. On 31 October, Manx youngsters have traditionally carried carved and lit turnips, known as 'moots', and gone from house to house reciting or (since the nineteenth century) singing some variant of this this odd poem:

> Hop-tu-naa, This is old Hollantide night,
> Trollalaa, The moon shines fair and bright.
> Hop-tu-naa, I went to the well,
> Trollalaa, And drank my fill;
> Hop-tu-naa, On the way coming back,
> Trollalaa, I met a pole-cat;
> Hop-tu-naa, The cat began to grin,
> Trollalaa, And I began to run;
> Hop-tu-naa, Where did you run to?
> Trollalaa, I ran to Scotland;
> Hop-tu-naa, What were they doing there?
> Trollalaa, Baking bannocks and roasting collops.
> Hop-tu-naa, If you are going to give us anything,
>   give us it soon,
> Or we'll be away by the light of the moon – Hop-tu-naa![29]

Money was exchanged for the performance, and the money was used to buy fireworks for Guy Fawkes Eve. Hop-tu-naa is still popular on the Isle of Man, although pumpkins are now as common as turnips, and Halloween material has been sold in shops for about the last decade. In one recent survey, 57 per cent of Manx residents reported that hop-tu-naa was 'still fairly active in several areas', although teenage respondents were more likely to use the name 'Halloween'.[30]

There were a few slightly more practical uses for Halloween as well. Folklore included many mentions of weather in reference to All Saints' Day because of its importance as a harvest festival and its place in the calendar as the transition from autumn to winter. One belief was that the wind's direction on Halloween would hold throughout winter. A more whimsical rhyme ran:

> If ducks do slide at Hollandtide, at Christmas they
> will swim;
> If ducks do swim at Hollandtide, at Christmas they
> will slide.[31]

The period between Halloween and Martinmas was often a short spell of warmer weather and was referred to by Shakespeare (in *Henry IV Part 1*) as 'All-Hallown Summer'. Farmers were commanded to sow wheat 'from Michaelmas to Hollandtide', and one recorded saying ran, 'Set trees at Allhallontide and command them to prosper; set them after Candlemas and entreat them to grow.'[32]

Just as the Celts had repaid debts on Samhain, so Halloween also had an economic side. It was a popular time for hiring fairs, when servants who had just finished another year's harvest with a lord would assemble to find next season's work. If these fairs were held on 2 November (All Souls' Day), they were sometimes referred to as 'soul-mass hirings'. Hiring fairs often included celebrations as well, since those hired were usually given a small advance payment. Hiring fairs also occurred on Guy Fawkes Day and Martinmas.

Edinburgh was famed for its annual Hallow-fair, which lasted for more than a week and is recorded in the Edinburgh Charter of 1507. Hallow-fair – which was still being held into the twenty-first century – was less about business (although much was conducted there) than it was about providing a final opportunity for fun before the onset of the cruel Scottish winter. The poet Robert Fergusson, sometimes thought of as the poet who paved the way for Burns, captured the atmosphere in his 'Hallow-fair' of 1772:

At Hallowmas, whan nights grow lang,
　　And starnies shine fu' clear,
Whan fock, the nippin cald to bang,
　　Their winter hap-warms wear,
Near Edinbrough a fair there hads,
　　I wat there's nane whase name is,
For strappin dames and sturdy lads,
　　And cap and stoup, mair famous
　　　　Than it that day.[33]

At Fergusson's Hallow-fair, young people drink and flirt, defy authority and buy goods from hawkers who have travelled long distances.

Hollantide fairs were also held in Wales, and were boisterous affairs with booths, crowded streets and pickpockets on the prowl. They involved both shopping – here, as in Scotland, gingerbread was a popular item – and hiring for the following year.

Charity was also a common fixture of the Halloween season. In Shropshire, for instance, All Saints' Day was celebrated with a tradition called either 'Pierce's Charity' or 'the parting of the white bread'. A gentleman named Pierce had specified in his will that a small amount should be set aside each year to prepare bread for local widows and widowers, and this custom continued until nearly the end of the nineteenth century.

One of the most curious Halloween business rituals was the Horseshoe and Hobnail Service, which took place in the law courts in London each 31 October until the turn of the twentieth century. Dating back roughly 700 years, this ritual involved payment of rent by the King's Remembrancer, acting on behalf of the tenants of two parcels of land held in Shropshire, to the Corporation of London, and consisted of two parts: first, the City Solicitor, acting on behalf of the Corporation, cut through two bundles of wood, using a hatchet on one and a bill-hook on the other; second, he counted out six horseshoes and 61 hobnails (the original rent due on the lands). This odd practice probably dated back to the use of the rented lands by the Knights Templar.

It was also around the end of the nineteenth century that the Catholic Church stopped naming churches 'Allhallows' out of deference to the growing popularity of Halloween. An account written in 1894 of a London parish named Allhallows Staining explains:

> The dedication, Allhallows, was in Pre-Reformation times a favourite one for churches. In later years a dedication of similar meaning, i.e., All Saints, has been preferred, and the term Allhallows is now usually restricted to All Hallows' Eve, 31st October.[34]

By the late nineteenth century, the celebration of Halloween in Great Britain seems to have been confined almost solely to children or poorer adults; virtually all of the descriptions of adult celebrations from this time describe the participants as 'servants', 'peasants' or 'beggars'.

Throughout much of the twentieth century, Halloween was little more than a curiosity in most of Britain, but over the last two decades, American-style Halloween has exploded in popularity throughout the UK. British retailers reported that UK Halloween spending went from £12 million in 2001 to £280 million in 2010,[35] with consumers purchasing pumpkins, decorations and costumes. Among the reasons given for the skyrocketing sales figures are the popularity of such U.S. films and series as *True Blood* and *Twilight*, and a desire to escape from a dismal economy into the realm of the fantastic.[36] While many modern Britons still celebrate Halloween with simple fireworks and parties, costumes are becoming more popular. The supermarket chain Tesco didn't even stock adult Halloween costumes until 2009, when the day fell on a Saturday, tipping off retailers to expect more sales. However, the bakery chain Greggs doubled sales of items such as bat biscuits and creepy cupcakes from 2008 to 2009. Another supermarket chain, Waitrose, reported a 676 per cent increase in sales of large pumpkins from 2009 to 2010. In 2009, retail sales for Halloween finally overtook those for Valentine's Day in the UK, and now lag behind only Easter and Christmas.[37]

How did a festival that was essentially born in the British Isles find new life there after more than a century of languishing as little more than a quaint memory? To answer that, it's necessary to leap across the Atlantic and examine how Halloween first took root in America during the nineteenth century, and why it came to flourish there.

3

Trick or Treat
in the New World

In 1845, a disease known as potato blight began to ravage the staple food crop of Ireland. Over the next seven years, approximately one million Irish would die, and another million left the country, many sailing to America. Scottish emigration to the United States was also high, with nearly half a million Scots settling in the New World during the latter half of the nineteenth century.

As these impoverished newcomers were crossing the Atlantic, changes were also occurring in the middle and upper classes on both sides of the ocean. Victoria ascended the throne in June 1837, and during her 65-year reign, Britain experienced prosperity, peace (for the most part) and significant advances in technology and medicine. In America, the influx of Scotch-Irish immigrants co-incided with the rise of the middle class, who were anxious to imitate their British cousins. Victoria herself spent Halloween in 1869 at Balmoral Castle in Scotland, and her experience there was widely reported:

> As the shades of evening were closing in . . . numbers of torchlights were observed approaching the castle . . . Dancing was commenced by the torch-bearers dancing a 'Huachan' in fine style, to the lilting strains of Mr Ross, the Queen's piper . . . After dancing for some time, the torch-bearers proceeded round the Castle in martial order, and as they were proceeding down the granite staircase at the northwest corner of the Castle, the procession presented a singularly beautiful

and romantic appearance. Having made the circuit of the Castle, the remainder of the torches were thrown in a pile at the south-west corner, thus forming a large bonfire, which was speedily augmented with other combustibles until it formed a burning mass of huge proportions, round which dancing was spiritedly carried on. Her Majesty witnessed the proceedings with apparent interest for some time . . . [1]

It's probably no coincidence that the first mentions of American Halloween celebrations began to appear shortly after this account, and were invariably linked to the growing middle class (albeit as a child's entertainment). A short story printed in a popular ladies' magazine of 1870 painted Halloween as an 'English' holiday celebrated by children, and describes a transplanted family's party in depth. As the children arrive, they must enter the house by stepping over a broom, placed there to keep witches out. The children tell fortunes by burning nuts, pouring hot lead into water and reading the shapes formed therein, laying out cards, and choosing among the luggie bowls (which have now been replaced by a basin of water, a pan of ashes and the wing of a goose, the last indicating marriage to an old man). The youthful revellers also play snapdragon (a game in which children try to snatch bits of dried fruit or wrapped fortunes from a dish of flaming alcohol), pull taffy and make 'fate cakes' (small cakes made in silence and then placed under the pillow to invoke dreams). Finally, the story's heroine, a young lady in love named Nell, walks backwards down the stairs only to be surprised by a kiss from her beau. The story limns Halloween as both charming and vaguely exotic, and after appearing in the popular *Godey's Lady's Book and Magazine*, it undoubtedly led to many copycat parties among its readers.

Some of the fortune-telling rituals that crossed the Atlantic remained popular in the New World long enough to take on a distinctly American flavour. Luggie bowls, for instance, are recorded at American parties as late as the Second World War, when they no longer held simply clean and dirty water, but were filled with red, white and blue-coloured water and named for different branches

of the armed services; thus a girl might discover the military affili-
ation of her future beloved. 'Kaling', nut-burning and apple-paring
all found a new home in America, usually with slight variations.

Immigrants brought other traditions with them as well, including some that were dying out in the Old World. Bonfires, for
instance, were held in America, albeit on a reduced scale. A *Good
Housekeeping* article of 1908 describes a Halloween party in which
boys were costumed as ghosts and placed around a bonfire, and
one boy dressed as the Devil pretended to grab them and throw
them into the flames.[2] It's easy to see why this did not become a
regular Halloween tradition.

Some customs were literally reversed on crossing the Atlantic:
in American versions of Halloween cabbage-pulling, the fortune-
seeker might be required to venture into the cabbage field backward.
A more ghoulish American version demanded that the seeker pass
through a graveyard on the way to the field. Cabbages also remained
popular in pranking, and in parts of Canada and the u.s., the night
before Halloween (which became the prime night for mischief) was
known as 'Cabbage Night' or 'Cabbage-stump Night', the latter
based on the practice of hurling cabbage stalks. Apples found favour
in America as well: apple juice became a standard item at Halloween celebrations, often served with doughnuts, popcorn and
pumpkin pie.

In America, the word 'corn' came to refer to maize, which is
harvested in late autumn. Corn-husking contests were sometimes
a feature of early American Halloween parties, and to this day
American Halloween decorations often include decorative ears of
corn (known as 'Indian corn') or corn stalks.

Another common American Halloween icon also derived from
the harvest: the scarecrow. Scarecrows, which are traditionally
figures made of old clothing and straw, serve an important function
throughout the growing year, driving birds away from crops; but
by late October, once the harvest has been completed, their useful-
ness is over. Despite 'Feathertop', Nathaniel Hawthorne's classic
tale of 1852 featuring a witch who brings a scarecrow to life, there's
little evidence that scarecrows figured prominently in Halloween

Contemporary Halloween scarecrow.

celebrations prior to 1900. It's likely that the scarecrow largely became a Halloween icon thanks to the efforts of early twentieth-century pranking boys, who frequently employed the figures in their night-time scares (often after replacing the head with a glowing jack-o'-lantern). Indeed, many of the early postcards that depict scarecrows either show them in the service of a mischievous young lad (who is usually holding it up behind a window to scare a girl), or show the would-be prankster being inadvertently frightened by his own creation. Scarecrows went on to become popular Halloween decorations, and folklorist Jack Santino has noted that, although sometimes referred to as 'harvest figures', they are almost always combined with Halloween imagery – witches, ghosts, skeletons, jack-o'-lanterns – in yard decoration, creating what he calls a 'folk assemblage'. They have also served as the basis of Halloween costumes and are popular scares in modern haunted attractions.

Towards the end of the nineteenth century, Halloween in America was in the process of acquiring what would become its most popular icon: the jack-o'-lantern carved from a pumpkin. The legend of Jack, the blacksmith who outwits the Devil, appears in hundreds of variants throughout both Europe and America, and typically ends when Jack dies and, being denied entrance to either Heaven or Hell, instead wanders the earth with his way lit only by an ember held in a carved-out turnip. In Britain, children had carved Halloween lanterns from large turnips or swedes, and in Scotland there are contemporary reports of masked youngsters carrying carved, lit turnips (called 'neep lanterns') and going from door to door asking, 'Please help the guisers.' At the village of Hinton St George in Somerset, a strange, Halloween-like festival called Punkie Night falls on the fourth Thursday of October, and involves children carving intricate designs into the skin of the mangelwurzel, a large beetroot-like vegetable normally grown as cattle feed. The children parade through the village streets singing this song:

> It's Punkie Night tonight,
> It's Punkie Night tonight,

Give us a candle, give us a light,
If you don't you'll get a fright.

It's Punkie Night tonight,
It's Punkie Night tonight,
Adam and Eve wouldn't believe
It's Punkie Night tonight.[3]

In America, pumpkins – the large, bright-orange squash native to the New World and harvested in late autumn – had been carved into grinning faces for decades prior to the arrival of Halloween. In 1820, Washington Irving immortalized the carved pumpkin in his story 'The Legend of Sleepy Hollow', and although the piece would later become a Halloween classic thanks to its combination of humour and fright, it made no direct mention of the day. In his poem 'The Pumpkin' of 1850, John Greenleaf Whittier links the pumpkin to another festival – Thanksgiving – but goes on to recall carving 'wild, ugly faces' in pumpkins lit from within by candles, and telling fairy stories by their light. Jack-o'-lanterns aren't mentioned in most of the Halloween party descriptions from the 1860s and '70s; an 1880 article suggests that they aren't even as useful as cabbages at Halloween. But within a few years, the legends of Jack the Blacksmith, Washington Irving's Ichabod Crane, turnip-carving from the Old World and the American tradition of cutting faces into the giant fruit would combine to create the jack-o'-lantern. In 1898, Martha Russell Orne, in her seminal pamphlet *Hallowe'en: How to Celebrate It*, suggested that a Halloween party should be 'grotesquely decorated with Jack-o'-lanterns made of apples, cucumbers, squashes, pumpkins, etc.' She also suggests creating 'bogies' from pumpkins:

A pumpkin is carefully hollowed out until nothing but the shell of the rind remains. One side of it is punctured with holes for the mouth, eyes, and nose, and made as nearly as possible to resemble a human face. A lighted candle is then fastened within, the eyebrows are put on with burnt-cork,

Jack-o'-lantern carving, postcard, *c.* 1910.

and a demon-like expression given to the features ... the
bogie is put in a dark room, where the young people may stray
on it unawares ...[4]

Orne's playful instructions seemed to catch on, not always to the
satisfaction of teachers, who by 1906 were complaining, 'Why
should these carved faces always be made so ugly?'[5] By the time of
Games for Hallowe'en (1912), jack-o'-lanterns specifically carved
from pumpkins were recommended for party decorations, table
decorations, lighting effects and games; jack-o'-lanterns of paste-
board 'should be made just large enough to fit over the gas jet' (in
this time prior to the widespread introduction of electricity).[6]

It wasn't until Halloween had become established in America
that it acquired most of its token animals. Only the cat had been
present in Halloween lore previously, and usually in association with
the witch. The Scots, for example, thought witches might turn cats
into horses to ride on Halloween night, while in America one folk
belief had it that a witch who boiled a live black cat on Halloween
night and then washed the bones in a spring would receive a visit
from the Devil, who would reveal to her the 'lucky bone' that would
henceforth serve as her talisman. Edgar Allan Poe's famed short
tale 'The Black Cat' is now a Halloween classic, even though it
makes no reference to the day itself, and cats figure prominently in
twentieth-century Halloween folk art. Cats have recently been a
source of concern at Halloween: in the USA black cats are believed
to be stolen for use in occult rituals, and many animal protection
agencies warn pet owners to keep close tabs on their black cats
during the Halloween season.

The tie between bats and owls and Halloween is less clear.
Both animals feature prominently in twentieth-century images of
the festival, but neither has any real association with it prior to
that; nor are they much mentioned in Celtic lore. It may be simply
that both are nocturnal predators (which could explain why spiders,
for example, are rarely featured in Halloween motifs). Bats may
also owe part of their enduring popularity to Bram Stoker's *Dracula*
(1897), since Stoker created the myth of the vampire's ability to

transform into a bat. It's also possible that the manufacturers of postcards and decorations who added the bat and the owl to Halloween iconography realized that many people genuinely found spiders and snakes too frightening to purchase in any form.

The only other animal featured prominently in nineteenth-century and earlier Halloween lore appeared virtually not at all from 1900 on: the horse. Horses, as the primary mode of transportation prior to the automobile, might carry witches, fairies or goblins on Halloween night. The Celts recorded horse racing as part of their Samhain festivities, and cavalcades were once a popular way to celebrate All Saints' Day. The pooka might transform into a horse, as in the story 'Mac-na-Michomhairle', about a pooka who takes that form and emerges from a hillside each Halloween, describing the events of the coming year to those who encounter it. Witches would use an enchanted bridle on Halloween to transform young men into steeds so they could engage in 'Hallowmass Rades', Scottish witch revels held on Halloween. In Britain, the ghostly 'Wild Hunt' (led by the 'Spectre Huntsman') was thought to be especially powerful on Halloween night, and was said to include twenty black horses and twenty black hounds.

Halloween's now-established colours of black and orange were also settled around this time. A few early twentieth-century Halloween decorating articles and guides suggest other colour schemes: for example, an article of 1912 on preparing a Halloween window decoration states that the day's colours are 'brown, yellow and white'.[7] However, an article from just six years later affirms absolutely that 'the colors for Hallowe'en are orange and black'.[8] The earlier colours had emphasized harvest, but now the jack-o'-lantern, night and death had come to dominate Halloween's colour palette.

As Halloween acquired emblems and a playful image, there was one area of the USA where Halloween was still celebrated as the more solemn All Saints' Day. The French who came to New Orleans and other parts of Louisiana brought their *La Toussaint* customs with them, and All Saints' Day was one of the most important days of the year in the nineteenth-century calendar. New

Orleans tourist guidebooks of the period always remark on the city's unique above-ground cemeteries, necessary because of the moist soil, and the 1 November celebrations that were considered one of the year's two great festivals, the other being Mardi Gras. Families visited the graves of departed loved ones and cleaned and decorated the monuments. Vendors lined up outside graveyards, offering flowers and food. By the end of the twentieth century, the New Orleans observance of All Saints' had considerably lessened, but nearby communities such as Lacombe and Lafitte were still vigorously celebrating with a night-time vigil, often conducted mainly by those of Creole descent. Louisiana remains the only state in America in which All Saints' Day is a legal holiday.

By the beginning of the 1900s, American Halloween celebrations were starting to transform again. This time they reinstated more of the pranking of Irish celebrations. In rural areas especially, 31 October soon became an evening that was almost exclusively celebrated by mischievous young boys. A turn-of-the-century guide on boys' crafts suggests:

This is the only evening on which a boy can feel free to play pranks outdoors without danger of being 'pinched,' and it is his delight to scare passing pedestrians, ring door-bells, and carry off the neighbors' gates (after seeing that his own is unhinged and safely placed in the barn). Even if he is suspected, and the next day made to remove the rubbish barricading the doors, lug back the stone carriage step, and climb a tree for the front gate, the punishment is nothing compared with the sports the pranks have furnished him.[9]

This same book goes on to describe methods for constructing 'bean-blowers' (aka pea-shooters), goblin figures and several varieties of the notorious 'tick-tack', an immensely popular Halloween noisemaker. This toy, which consisted of a notched wooden spool on a stick, could be run over windows to create a startling loud rattle, and for almost half a century the tick-tack was practically synonymous with Halloween.

The Halloween black cat, postcard, *c.* 1910.

Not everyone saw Halloween mischief as simply the fun-loving but ultimately harmless sport of young boys. As pranking became more widespread, it became more of a problem. Simply disassembling a gate – in fact, the name 'Gate Night' replaced Halloween in many areas – was one thing, but disassembling the gate and then moving it into the centre of town where it might be piled in the middle of Main Street with dozens of other gates was more troublesome. In the 1920s, Halloween pranking spread into the rapidly expanding major urban areas, and became out-and-out vandalism. Although the simple pranks of the past – switching shop signs, or flinging a sock filled with flour at a man's black coat – were still practised, so were far more destructive activities, including breaking windows, tripping pedestrians and setting fires. In 1933, during the height of America's Great Depression, destructive Halloween prank-playing was so virulent that many cities dubbed that year's celebration 'Black Halloween'. Vandalism was now described as the work of 'hoodlums' rather than mischievous boys, and included sawing down telephone poles, overturning automobiles, opening fire hydrants to flood city streets and openly

Emile Friant, *All Saints' Day*, 1888, oil on canvas.

taunting the police. Local governments that were already struggling economically were overwhelmed, and many considered banning Halloween altogether.

Fortunately, more practical alternatives proved to be effective: towns and civic groups such as the YMCA and the Boy Scouts began to offer boys other ways to celebrate Halloween, including parties, parades, costuming, carnivals and contests. Schools took an active role in entertaining children at Halloween, and soon there was an entire cottage industry based around writing holiday booklets aimed specifically at children and teachers. These books were popular from about 1915 until 1950 (when trick or treat took over, in other words), and included poetry recitations, one-act plays, pageant suggestions and other theatrical performances that would presumably occupy young minds for the week leading up to Halloween, and would thus keep them from contemplating pranking. Some of these pieces, in fact, specifically addressed the problem of pranking, albeit in a charming manner that theoretically would appeal to children. Take, for example, the short play 'Making Jack-o'-lanterns' from *The Best Halloween Book* (1931), which includes this dialogue between two boys as they work on their pumpkins:

> HAROLD. I think I'll go over the tracks and scare the Widow Mitchell a little. We did that last year and had a lot of fun.
>
> BILL. It wasn't so much fun when she told the principal about it and we all lost our recesses. Let's think of something different.
>
> HAROLD. I'd like to do something with mine that would bring pleasure to some one instead of injury. There must be some good that can be done with jack-o'-lanterns.[10]

After Harold's abrupt change of heart, the boys decide to present their jack-o'-lanterns to a poor family that cannot afford their own.

Chambers of commerce and other merchant associations also took an active part in distracting would-be Halloween pranksters.

An article of 1939 that appeared in an official publication of the Rotary Club touted decreased pranking (due in part, of course, to activities sponsored by Rotary Clubs across the USA), and described how store-owners had succeeded with everything from paying for parties to bringing rowdy boys to a boxing ring on Halloween night. Rotarians in Calexico, California, described their Halloween 'mirthquake':

> First, a noise parade of costumed school children led by their teachers; next, an interval of field contests – tugs of war, a sandbag race, a fifth-grade football classic; a greased-pig-catching contest – then free tickets to a theater.[11]

Window-decorating contests, costume contests and even renting trains to carry rural pranksters to town were all cheaper than repairing mass vandalism, and youngsters seemed eager to participate as well.

One town took the pranking problem so seriously that it ended up becoming the town's identity: Anoka, Minnesota, claims to have been 'the first city in the United States to put on a Halloween celebration to divert its youngsters from Halloween pranks'. Tired of waking up on 1 November to find their cattle roaming on Main Street, in 1920, Anoka's civic leaders instituted a programme of Halloween parades, giveaways and bonfires. In 1937, twelve-year-old Harold Blair arrived in Washington, DC, with a proclamation naming Anoka 'the Halloween Capital of the World'. The insignia on Harold's sweater is now embedded in one of Anoka's downtown sidewalks, and the town has continued to hold both the title and the celebrations. A combination of parades and contests spans the week preceding Halloween and boasts 40,000 participants.

While teachers kept troublemakers occupied in school and merchants made towns safe again, parents created diversions at home for their mischievous offspring. Thanks to the Depression, however, money in the late 1920s and early '30s was scarce, and parties weren't cheap. One solution was for neighbours to pool resources and create the 'house-to-house party' in which groups

An Anoka Halloween
button from 2007.

of children were led from one house to the next, each home host-ing a different themed activity. This would soon evolve into another tradition, perhaps the most cherished of all American Halloween rituals.

Trick or Treat

While it's tempting to draw connections between the New World's institutionalized begging ritual and earlier, Old World traditions such as the masked house-to-house performances of the Grülacks or the Strawboys, Guy Fawkes begging or souling, trick or treat probably sprang out of more recent antecedents. In New York City, Thanksgiving, now celebrated in the USA with a traditional turkey dinner on the fourth Thursday of November, was compared in the 1870s with Guy Fawkes Day. It had become a rowdy festival of thousands of boys organized in crews (similar to the Guy Fawkes crews who still parade in Lewes each year), who were rewarded with gifts of money. Costumed children were also recorded going from house to house and begging food.

Even more similar to trick or treating was a Christmas custom called 'belsnickling'. Derived from a German mumming tradition known as *Peltztnickel*, belsnickling was performed in the eastern areas of the USA and Canada, and consisted of groups of costumed participants moving from house to house, offering small 'tricks' in exchange for treats of food and drink. In Nova Scotia, the belsnickling performers deliberately frightened young children, who might be asked if they had been good before being rewarded with a treat. In one version of belsnickling, those whose houses were visited by the costumed revellers were required to guess the identities of the disguised guests, and had to hand over a treat to anyone they couldn't identify; this same custom appears in some early descriptions of trick or treat, lending credence to the possibility that it derived from its Christmas cousin. In fact, the earliest recorded usage of the actual phrase 'trick or treat' in connection with Halloween comes from Alberta, Canada, where in 1927 a newspaper article reported on pranksters demanding 'trick or treat' at houses (although no mention of costuming is made). By the 1930s, the phrase in connection with Halloween and costumed children seemed to be working its way down through the northern USA, as states like Oregon reported that 'young goblins and ghosts, employing modern shakedown methods, successfully worked the 'trick or treat' system'.[12] One of the first national mentions of trick or treat appears in an article of 1939 entitled 'A Victim of the Window-Soaping Brigade?', which both refers to 'trick or treat' as 'the age-old Halloween salutation' and makes it plain that the practice was a method of subverting rowdy pranking.[13] Still, it wasn't until after the Second World War – when rationing was over and luxuries like candy were once again readily available – that trick or treat finally spread throughout the entire USA.

As trick or treat replaced pranking, it seemed that the day now belonged almost entirely to pre-pubescents. Adults might occasionally dress in costume for parties, but for the most part they were expected to spend Halloween passing out candy to masked children. How was it that even the young adults of Robert Burns's classic poem no longer actively celebrated the day?

The answer to that may best be found in two unexpected areas: retailing and Prohibition.

The Edwardian era was prosperous, and leisure activities were plentiful. In the Victorian age, Halloween parties for youngsters had involved a considerable amount of adult participation: invitations, costumes and decorations were made days in advance and required the knowhow of mothers and fathers. But as the twentieth century dawned, paper goods companies catering to party-giving hostesses sprang up, and by the 1910s companies like Beistle and B. Shackman had begun to produce and import pre-made decorations, taking some of the burden off adults. Dozens of small booklets outlining activities for Halloween parties were published, and the Dennison Company introduced a line of annual decorating guides called *Bogie Books* that gave detailed instructions on how to use Dennison products to quickly and attractively decorate for Halloween parties. For about a decade, Halloween parties for adults were probably as popular as those for children, with the latter being held in the afternoons and early evenings to accommodate the later gathering for the adults.

Then, in 1919, the u.s. Congress passed the Eighteenth Amendment to the Constitution, and liquor was banned – or at least driven into the shadowy haven of speakeasies. Although Dennison continued to publish the *Bogie Books*, adult participation in parties took a serious blow when liquor became absent.

By this time, though, Halloween had become too popular to die easily. In the era between gas and electricity, between communicating via letters and the widespread use of telephones, one artistic form of staying in touch blossomed: picture postcards. Postcards were printed celebrating places, people and events, and holidays were no exception. During this golden age of postcards, over 3,000 Halloween cards were produced, and the fantastical, colourful design of these cards worked to codify and solidify Halloween iconography. Jack-o'-lanterns were featured prominently, often anthropomorphized into playful vegetable-headed men; the seasonal, merry orange fruit even appeared on some cards in the costume of a king, showing how the pumpkin had risen to prominence as

Vintage postcard that seems to be a parody of the popular character 'Buster Brown', *c.* 1910.

Halloween's leading icon. Depictions of witches were plentiful, taking two forms: the classic wizened hag bent over a bubbling cauldron, attended by a faithful black cat (and possibly servile imps), or the lovely young, heavily sexualized witch, often dressed in crimson and seated on a broom. However, though the witch, black cat and jack-o'-lantern all sound like images of the modern Halloween, these cards still show a festival in transition, as many of them depict the fortune-telling games still being played at parties of the time.

By the 1930s, another popular graphic art aimed at adults was capitalizing on Halloween: the pin-up. Hollywood studios frequently presented their attractive starlets in provocative outfits as they

A youthful witch
on Halloween,
postcard, *c.* 1910.

posed for leading photographers, and for October the ingénues
might be dressed as witches or posed with pumpkins. During the
Second World War, the popularity of pin-ups increased, thanks to
overseas servicemen who were hungry for a glimpse of anything
female, and Halloween pin-ups occasionally incorporated military
imagery as well.

Overall, though, the period between the two World Wars saw
Halloween move through a cycle from adult and children's parties
to pranking to ritualized trick or treat. During the Second World

War, rationing put a slight dampener on the home celebrations, but when the war finally ended, trick or treat had infiltrated virtually every area of America, spurred on by a huge boom in developing new suburban neighbourhoods. It had become the pre-eminent activity of Halloween. The fortune-telling customs of earlier eras were discarded, and the young people who had once enjoyed practising those games were now confined to either the occasional costume party or handing out treats with older family members.

In the 1940s and '50s, Halloween imagery and merchandising changed to reflect the new institution of trick or treat. The *Bogie Books* ceased publication in 1934, and the popularity of postcards declined sharply as telephones became commonplace (just as the heyday of pin-ups passed with the end of the Second World War). The new retailing trends catered to trick or treat, and so emphasized candy and costumes. In the past, costumes had been relatively simple homemade affairs, and had often utilized the image of the outsider: costumes for gypsies, hobos, bandits and pirates were all easy to produce, requiring little more than old castoff clothing and a few accessories. However, as manufacturing techniques changed in the 1950s and facilitated silkscreening on cheap rayon or vinyl, and as plastic production allowed the creation of inexpensive, colourful masks, shop-bought costumes began to replace the traditional homemade outfits. The popularity of the new medium of television was exploding, and costume manufacturers played on this, licensing such beloved small-screen figures as Howdy Doody, Kukla and Ollie, and comedienne Lucille Ball. Old favourites like witches and ghosts were still popular, but a ghost costume made simply from a white sheet was passé, as mass-produced ghost costumes included ghoulish masks and costumes featuring stylized, colourful graphics. The new costumes were safer, too, made from flame-retardant materials. In the past, too many children had suffered as a result of parading in flowing costumes with lit lanterns, as was the case with four-year-old starlet Caryll Ann Ekelund, who had appeared in the Shirley Temple film *The Blue Bird* and who died in 1939 after her Halloween costume caught fire from a jack-o'-lantern. Unfortunately, every Halloween still sees reports of revellers who become burn victims after a homemade costume catches fire.

Candy companies didn't really begin to target Halloween heavily until trick or treat. Candy had first made its appearance at American Halloween parties in the form of taffy that children could pull as part of the entertainment. The first mass-produced candies that were popular at Halloween were tiny sugar pellets that served mainly to fill festive, brightly coloured containers. However, a candy first manufactured in the 1880s and finally mass-produced in the 1920s would soon become the preferred Halloween sweet: candy corn. Originally designed to imitate an individual corn kernel, its festive colours (orange, yellow and white) and cone shape captivated consumers. The colours and corn shape connected it with autumn and harvest, and soon that connection led to the autumn's main candy purchasing event, Halloween. Candy corn is still a favourite American Halloween item, now produced largely by Brach's Candy Company, who estimate that Halloween accounts for three-quarters of its annual candy corn sales. Candy corn's design has led to both a panoply of spin-off products for Halloween, including costumes and candles, and candy corn produced in the colours of other celebrations, such as 'reindeer corn' in red, white and green for Christmas. Candy corn has even inspired its own day: 30 October is (in the USA, at least) National Candy Corn Day.

As trick or treat's popularity exploded in the post-Second World War era, adults found it far easier to hand out individually wrapped sweets than the apples, nuts, popcorn balls and homemade candies that had been given out in earlier days. Despite the perennial popularity of candy corn, chocolate soon became the preferred sugary treat. By the late 2000s, Halloween – after lagging behind Valentine's Day and Easter for decades – finally became the top U.S. holiday in terms of chocolate sales, with sales in 2009 reported at 598 million pounds of candy earning $1.9 billion in sales.[14] Leading manufacturers Hershey's, Mars and M&Ms not only began to produce new products specifically for the Halloween season, but for some time have been creating very specific

Halloween-themed marketing campaigns. As Hershey's spokesperson Jody Cook notes:

All holidays are important, but we strive to make people think of Hershey's when they think of Halloween. Every year we come out with new packaging, designs or products to keep the excitement around what Hershey's is offering.[15]

By the 1950s, other industries had begun to capitalize on trick or treat as well: grocers printed branded trick or treat bags, meat

A supermarket Halloween candy display in 2011.

producers gave out kits and booklets that included cut-out masks, motion picture and television companies produced Halloween cartoons and episodes, and even adult products like cigarettes featured trick or treat and Halloween imagery in their magazine and newspaper print ads.

Two of the most popular accessories for any trick or treating child were the jack-o'-lantern treat collector and the noisemaker. In the past, children venturing between houses on a dark October night might have carried a small papier mâché jack-o'-lantern holding a candle within; by the 1950s, trick or treaters in need of illumination could be equipped with plastic battery-operated pumpkins that also served as treat collectors. Finally, the illuminated aspect of the plastic pumpkins was dropped altogether in favour of a large, lightweight treat container.

Noisemakers were the descendants of the tick-tack. Where earlier sound-producing toys had largely been homemade out of wood (the 'horse fiddle', which consisted of a wooden wheel with four or five wooden slats spun around it, was another popular creation), the new noisemakers were mass-produced in metal and featured eye-popping graphics in vivid hues. Trick or treaters had the option of very loudly announcing their arrival at a house by shaking a rattle, banging a tambourine, blowing a horn, squeezing a clicker or cranking a ratchet. Carl B. Holmberg, an Associate Professor of Popular Culture at Bowling Green State University, has suggested that noisemakers provided children with 'ritual empowerment' by allowing them to produce the irritating loud sounds they were normally forbidden from making. Holmberg also indicates that the use of Halloween noisemakers faded as they were supplanted by 'atmospheric' sounds: that is, homeowners who began to include prerecorded sound effects and spooky music with their seasonal yard displays.[16] However, the use of Halloween noisemakers has recently returned in the haunted attraction industry, as actors working in Halloween mazes are now frequently supplied with either simple noisemakers, such as tin cans full of coins, or higher-tech devices, like special gloves with steel plates.

Vintage Halloween
'clapper' noisemaker,
c. 1950.

Noisemakers were not the only sign that trick or treat had not
been entirely successful in stifling the pranksters' spirits. In the
mid-twentieth century a new phenomenon appeared: pranking
on 30 October, the night before Halloween. It's hard to pinpoint
exactly when or where this new custom began, but it's probably no
coincidence that there are almost no references to it prior to the
1940s – when trick or treat arose, in other words. Displaced pranking found a new home on the thirtieth, and under a variety of names,
including 'Devil's Night', 'Goosey Night', 'Mischief Night', 'Cabbage
Night' and 'Damage Night'. There are nineteenth-century British

references to Mischief Night, but they refer to 30 April, not 30 October, even though the description is startlingly similar:

> All kinds of mischief were then perpetrated; water-tubs were overturned, door handles tied securely fast, shopkeepers' signboards exchanged, and other unmentionable freaks performed, until the establishment of regular police put an end to these vagaries.[17]

Mischief Night has more recently referred in Great Britain to 4 November, the night before Guy Fawkes Day. The name Devil's Night is now most associated with the city of Detroit, Michigan, where it led to massive instances of arson in the 1980s (297 Devil's Night fires were recorded in the city in 1984). In the mid-1990s, a combination of urban renewal and volunteer efforts brought Detroit's arson problem under control, but other cities have also reported multiple incidences of arson on 30 October, including some in Great Britain. Mischief Night/Devil's Night crimes have also recently been linked to racial tensions.

Trick or treat also had a positive side effect for at least one charity: in 1950, an American couple convinced a few neighbourhood children to collect money for the United Nations International Children's Emergency Fund (UNICEF), and the practice became so popular that in 1967, President Lyndon B. Johnson named 31 October National UNICEF Day. The UNICEF trick or treat programme remains popular, and has helped raise relief funds for such recent disasters as the Indian Ocean tsunami and Hurricane Katrina. UNICEF also touts 'the extraordinary empowerment and pride a child experiences' while securing donations during trick or treating.[18]

Certainly the empowerment aspect of trick or treat was a large part of why it became such a popular annual pastime for many children. Charity aside, for one night a year, American youngsters were allowed to put aside their usual identity, encouraged to become a beloved character, allowed to parade around after dark and make noise, and be rewarded by adults. It's probably no coincidence that trick or treat shot to prominence in the 1950s, the same decade in

Costumed adults dispense candy to trick-or-treaters in Beverly Hills, California.

which over-protective parents and crusading psychologists began to complain about violent comic books and rock 'n' roll. Halloween guaranteed children at least a small release from repression, even if only for one night.

So did what author David J. Skal has called 'Monster Culture'.[19] In October 1957, Screen Gems released to television a package of 52 horror films from Universal; the blanket title was 'Shock Theater', and the roster included such classics as *Frankenstein*, *The Bride of Frankenstein*, *Dracula*, *The Mummy* and *The Wolfman*. A year later, an agent and horror movie collector named Forrest J. Ackerman began editing a magazine called *Famous Monsters of Filmland*, which featured short pieces on various horror films and was heavily illustrated with photos culled from Ackerman's extensive collection. 'Monster Culture' was generated, and soon Halloween was awash with Dracula, Frankenstein and other monster movie masks and costumes. A night out trick or treating often ended with returning home for a monster movie, and 'Monster Culture' also led to such influential Halloween works as Bobby 'Boris' Pickett's hit song 'Monster Mash' of 1962, and the rise of the horror show host or hostess. 'Monster Culture' has also contributed heavily to Halloween haunted houses, and has even resulted in one attraction dedicated solely to the classic movie monsters: Cortlandt B. Hull's Witch's Dungeon Classic Movie Museum in Bristol, Connecticut, which features detailed life-sized recreations of Boris Karloff as Frankenstein's monster, Bela Lugosi's Dracula, Lon Chaney Sr as the Phantom of the Opera, and even Hull's great-uncle Henry Hull as the eponymous lead of 1935's *Werewolf of London*.

Given trick or treat's almost universal suburban popularity, its emphasis on representations of outsiders, and the way it empowered its participants, it was perhaps inevitable that trick or treat was about to experience a backlash. Adults, it seemed, were unwilling to grant their children that power after all.

In 1964, a New York housewife named Helen Pfeil was upset at the number of trick or treaters whom she thought were too old to be demanding candy, and handed them packages of dog biscuits, poisonous ant buttons and steel wool. Within three years the urban legend of children being given apples with hidden razor blades surfaced, and parents began to worry about Halloween. Stories of anonymous psychos hiding everything from arsenic to LSD in Halloween treats became rampant, especially following the case of eight-year-old Timothy Mark O'Bryan, who died in 1974 after eating a cyanide-laced 'Pixie Stix'. That little Timothy's murder was eventually linked to his father, Ronald Clark O'Bryan, didn't matter in the public imagination; the fear of the madman who was out to poison children on Halloween had already been introduced.

Trick or treat, however, refused to die. Alternatives were soon found: hospitals provided services on Halloween night to check children's candy, even going so far as to offer the use of their x-ray machines. Shopping malls and merchants capitalized on the fear by giving out Halloween treats and promoting a 'safe environment' for children. Local zoos created trick or treat events, with stations set up around their grounds to provide different treats. And educational programmes taught children to throw away any unwrapped treats, including apples and nuts.

As trick or treat became more gentrified, folklorists and sociologists heatedly debated its merits. In his essay 'Trick or Treat: Pre-texts and Contexts', Tad Tuleja notes how children now often costume themselves in the packaging of a favourite food or product, and adds:

> Far from encouraging communalism or redistribution, the ritual certifies, and even models, competitive vigor: the successful trick-or-treater is a budding entrepreneur, whose packaging and legwork have provided personal income.[20]

If, by the twenty-first century, the average American child couldn't even explain the 'trick' part of the phrase 'trick or treat', this was not the case in Britain. As trick or treat began to increase in popularity in Britain, so did pranking. In fact, in 2004 the British supermarket chain Asda decided to ban sales of eggs to teenagers in the weeks leading up to Halloween. 'We've said that we're going to be more vigilant and we're not going to be selling eggs to under-16s', stated a spokesperson for the giant retailer.[21]

Halloween for Adults

As trick or treat was beginning to decline, or at least to be brought under (corporate) control, other factors were also beginning to tilt Halloween celebrations back towards focusing on adults. Many of the baby boomers who had been so fond of trick or treating as youngsters – specifically, those who had been children in the 1950s, the golden age of trick or treat – seemed reluctant to give up celebrating it. And in the 1970s, as peoples of colour, women and gays sought equal rights, Halloween was inevitably pulled into the quest for progress.

Halloween has had a long and difficult history in regards to non-whites, especially African Americans. In the 1920s, when African Americans were stereotyped as easily frightened and superstitious, Halloween books suggested parties, costumes and decorations featuring 'darkies', 'mammy' or 'rastus'. Even Halloween books aimed primarily at children perpetuated racist stereotypes – 1936's *Halloween Fun Book*, which features recitations, plays, songs and games for children, includes a poem entitled 'A Darky's Halloween',

From the *Jocular Jinks of Kornelia Kinks'* series of postcards: 'Gran'pa done say dat his face it am old / So I'se give him dis new one and hopes he won't scold', 1907.

written in exaggerated dialect and depicting a pair of African Americans as 'two little darkies half-dead with fright, / Who had forgotten 'twas Halloween night'.[22] The Ku Klux Klan, when brought before Congress in 1921, tried to equate their tall, pointed cowls to Halloween masks.[23] In a 1965 hearing, they stated that their tactics of harassment and vandalism 'should always have a humorous twist . . . and should be in the nature of Halloween pranks'.[24] Throughout the twentieth century, there are incidents of Halloween rowdyism that led to crimes perpetrated by whites against blacks. Sometimes, as in the Halloween murder of a young African American man in Corinth, Mississippi, in 1959, months of racial violence and tension followed. Halloween racism continued into the twenty-first century: in 2001, white students at Auburn University in Alabama held a Halloween party in which they dressed as members of the Ku Klux Klan and staged the lynchings of other white students in blackface. After they posted photos on the Internet, 185 students were suspended.

One incident from Southern California's Long Beach area put a different spin on Halloween racial tensions in 2006: on Halloween night, three white women aged between nineteen and twenty-one who were visiting a neighbourhood known for its extravagant Halloween decorations were attacked by a number of black teenagers who hurled pumpkins and racial epithets. Eventually eight defendants were convicted of felony assault with a hate-crime enhancement (a ninth was convicted only of assault), and sentenced to probation and house arrest.

Halloween and gay culture, however, seem to have been a far more convivial mix. The celebration, of course, had always been a sanctuary for cross-dressers. Note, for example, these lines from Charles Frederick White's poem 'Hallowe'en' of 1908: 'The women dressed in men's attire / The small girl, too, quenched her desire / To get into her brother's pants'.[25] By the late 1930s, nightclubs around the u.s. were holding Halloween contests for 'female impersonators'. However, it wasn't until the 1970s – just a few years after the Stonewall riots in Greenwich Village, a pivotal moment in the history of the gay rights movement – that the Greenwich Village parade began and quickly brought gay participation in Halloween into the spotlight. In 1991, in an essay about the parade, folklorist Jack Kugelmass noted, Halloween's 'recent revival as an American adult festival speaks less to the possibility of religious enchantment than it does to the license the event provides',[26] and certainly in the 1980s the Village Halloween Parade emerged as a decadent festival of Mardi Gras-like proportions. Begun in 1973 by puppeteer Ralph Lee, the parade's proximity to Christopher Street, the heart of New York's gay culture, practically ensured that gay participation in the event would grow. On any given Halloween, among the parade's 60,000 marchers will be drag queens, large articulated puppets, marching bands and every conceivable costume from gladiators to religious figures to giant walking condoms. The event, which draws two million attendees and is viewed on television by another million, bills itself as 'the nation's largest public Halloween celebration' and has become a major cultural landmark for New York. In recent years, the parade has sought to convey a more family-friendly image, emphasizing a 'safe, celebrative environment'.[27]

But gay-oriented Halloween celebrations have hardly been confined to New York: Southern California's West Hollywood began its own 'carnaval' in 1987, and the Halloween event now draws half a million visitors. The community blocks off a lengthy section of Santa Monica Boulevard and holds live musical performances and contests, although most of the festivities are confined to gawking at the amazing array of costumes.

San Francisco's history of gay-themed Halloween celebrations has been somewhat more troubled. Prior to the 1980s, most of the festivities involved drag queens and their escorts going from bar to bar to display their complicated costumes. However, as the event migrated to Castro Street and grew in size, so did the attendance of 'fag-bashers', or anti-gay protesters. The city tried to counter this by offering its own official party, which only resulted in two distinct celebrations occurring simultaneously. Unfortunately, the Castro celebrations continued to result in violence, and after a gunman opened fire in 2006, wounding nine, authorities began to practice a 'zero tolerance policy' on Halloween night.

Another group on the fringe of American culture has also claimed Halloween for itself: Wiccans and neo-pagans. In contrast to the stereotypical (largely Catholic and medieval) portrayal of the witch as a minion of Satan, modern witches, who returned to the root word *wicce* when they named themselves, tend to follow a belief system that is benevolent, centred in earth worship and free of infant sacrifice. There are also a wide variety of other neo-pagan beliefs, all of which are polytheistic and which include Shamanism, Druidism and systems based on Norse or Egyptian beliefs. The modern neo-pagan movement first began to organize in the 1960s, and came to public awareness with the publication of Margot Adler's influential study *Drawing Down the Moon* (1979).

Because the term 'neo-pagan' encompasses so many different belief systems, there are a wide range of practices on 31 October. Halloween is a major festival for most neo-pagans, and may be referred to as 'Shadowfest', 'Ancestor Night' or Samhain; it's typically a New Year's celebration, although some groups – such as Druids – may reserve the winter solstice for that occasion. For Wiccans, 31 October is one of the eight major Sabbats, and is celebrated with a ritual that acknowledges both the presence of the ancestors and the transfer of power from the Mother Goddess (who rules during summer) to the God, who will hold sway until the following Beltane (1 May). Wiccans may also incorporate modern Halloween iconography such as the jack-o'-lantern into their rituals, and follow the more solemn observation with a festive party. Many neo-pagan groups celebrate around bonfires, and acknowledgement of deceased loved ones usually plays an important role in celebration. The spirits may be called to join in the festivities, or devices such as crystal balls and scrying mirrors may be employed in an attempt to communicate with those who have passed beyond. Most neo-pagan groups also have special foods, herbs and stones associated with the festival.

Wiccans also created their own Halloween mecca: Salem, Massachusetts, now hosts one of the largest community-wide Halloween celebrations in the world. In 1692, Salem was the site of one of the most famous witch trials in history – nineteen people were hanged as witches, and the trials served as the inspiration for

Arthur Miller's classic commentary on 1950s McCarthyism, *The Crucible*. Salem became inextricably linked with the word 'witch', and in 1971 Laurie Cabot opened the first shop in Salem specializing in Wiccan materials. In 1982, the Salem Chamber of Commerce inaugurated 'Haunted Happenings', a weekend-long celebration of Halloween that exceeded expectations; now, area hotels book up a year in advance, and Wiccans continue to be a significant part of the event. Salem has built on the notion of being a 'magical' destination, especially at Halloween. Christian Day, a witch and the owner of the Salem shop Hex, suggests that people are drawn to Salem at Halloween 'because they want magic in their lives'.[28]

The 'Haunted Happenings' now extend for the entire month of October and include tours, cruises, film screenings, street markets, celebrity appearances, séances, magic lessons and trick or treat for children, performed excerpts from *The Crucible* and Samhain rituals on 31 October. The 'Haunted Happenings' website also lists 'Year-round Halloween attractions in Salem', which include murseums, galleries and tours.

Trial of George Jacobs of Salem for witchcraft.

The adult reclamation of Halloween that took place in the 1970s culminated not with a group based on ethnicity, sexual orientation or religious belief, but with a single film. In 1979, a low-budget thriller grabbed moviegoers all over the world by the throat: John Carpenter's *Halloween* did not just become one of the most successful independent films ever made and the progenitor of a whole new sub-genre – the slasher film – but also presented Halloween in such a terrifying light that it was a wonder anyone would want to celebrate it after seeing the film. Carpenter's movie, based on ideas by producer Irwin Yablans and a script Carpenter co-wrote with Debra Hill, created two iconic characters: Michael Myers, the silent killer who escapes from a mental institution during Halloween and wreaks havoc on his hometown of Haddonfield, Illinois; and Laurie Strode, the virginal and resourceful 'final girl' who manages to survive Michael's rampage. The film played knowingly on its viewers' affection for Halloween by incorporating pumpkins, costumes, masks, popcorn, scary movies on television, children and suburbia; but whereas films like Steven Spielberg's *E.T.: The Extra-Terrestrial* (1982) painted Halloween with a warm, nostalgic glow, *Halloween* turned beloved icons into signifiers of terror. A young boy's clown costume was now what the pre-adolescent Michael Myers wore on his first massacre; a jack-o'-lantern wielded a knife on the film's one-sheet poster; and – in the strangest and funniest twist – a rubber mask of *Star Trek* actor William Shatner became a killer's menacing disguise. *Halloween* spawned not only its own sequels and remakes, but an entire cycle of 'holiday' horror films, including *My Bloody Valentine, April Fool's Day* and of course *Friday the 13th*. None of those films, however, could boast such adept use of a festival's imagery, or such an impact on the celebration they purloined.

Throughout the 1980s, trick or treat continued to limp along, but there was no question that Halloween had arrived as an adult festival. In 1983, America's third-place beer company, Coors, decided to counter their competitors' sales on Super Bowl Sunday and Memorial Day by 'creating a new beer holiday'.[29] Their first two Halloween campaigns (which featured the forgettable 'BeerWolf' and 'Silver Bullet Bar') were hardly runaway smashes, but in 1986

German lobby card from Carpenter's *Halloween*.

they hit on the formula for success by hiring 'Elvira', the curvaceous horror-movie hostess played by comedienne Cassandra Peterson. Fuelled by life-size cardboard cutouts of Elvira (which were frequently stolen by store employees), Coors sales surged, and by 1995 Elvira had gained the moniker 'Queen of Halloween'. Thanks to the Coors/Elvira campaign, Halloween had soon surpassed Super Bowl Sunday and St Patrick's Day in beer sales.

Halloween wasn't only being reclaimed by urban adults, however; suburban homeowners were also making it their own by investing heavily in decorations. In the past, decorations had been simple and hand-crafted. A few carved pumpkins, perhaps a scarecrow and some hay bales (more representative of Halloween as a harvest celebration than a horror celebration), and some cutout figures had been the extent of most yard displays. Companies like Beistle and Dennison offered a small yearly selection of cut-out figures (black cats, skeletons, and witches were the most popular), banners and window decals. A few enterprising souls went further, adding some hanging ghosts made from sheets, tombstones carved from wood or Styrofoam, or, for the very ambitious, actual mannequins turned into monsters or corpses. But for the most part, Halloween lagged far behind Christmas in terms of home and yard decorations.

But in the 1980s, as Halloween surged in popularity with adults, it also became more commercialized. Extravagant decorations began to appear in drug stores and supermarkets, and decorations got a big boost in 1983 with the appearance of Halloween seasonal stores. That year, a San Francisco dress shop owner named Joseph Marver decided to fill in his October slump by offering costumes, and the business was an immediate hit. The following year he rented a temporary space in a mall, and his sales went through the roof. Thus were born the seasonal Spirit Halloween Stores, which Marver sold to Spencer Gifts in 1999, and which operated over 900 stores in 2011. Although Marver started with costumes, the Spirit stores (and other seasonal Halloween stores) soon expanded to include home decorations, and homeowners began to take the same interest in Halloween decorating that they had traditionally shown at Christmas. Adult interest in Halloween was also spurred on by the mass merchandising of such popular media franchises as *Star Wars*,

A Spirit Halloween store, Burbank, California, 2011.

Star Trek and of course *Halloween* and *A Nightmare on Elm Street*, and soon parents could dress their tot in a *Smurfs* costume and decorate their yard with a realistic life-size figure of Freddy Kruger. By 1999, almost 30 per cent of America's consumers spent money on Halloween decorations, and in 2001 Americans spent nearly $1 billion on them.

Many of these home decorators weren't just creating a casual display in their yards: instead they were putting on actual walk-through shows, with miniature versions of the mazes that had begun to appear during the Halloween season in the 1970s. And as homeowners began to produce more and more elaborate seasonal displays, so did the more professional maze producers. In fact, what no one foresaw in the 1980s – or even the early 1990s – was another transformation in Halloween that was just around the corner. By the twenty-first century, Halloween would still be celebrated with trick or treat, parties and yard decorations, but it would also become virtually a global industry.

Halloween Haunts

It's hard to pinpoint the exact origins of what is now known as the 'haunted attractions industry', but it probably had its rough beginnings in the 1930s, when parents, anxious to divert the attention of pranking boys, created events like 'trails of terror'. This description of a 'trail of terror' from a party pamphlet of 1937 sounds uncannily similar to scenes that are standard in contemporary haunted houses:

> An outside entrance leads to a rendezvous with ghosts and witches in the cellar or attic. Hang old fur, strips of raw liver on walls, where one feels his way to dark steps ... Weird moans and howls come from dark corners, damp sponges and hair nets hung from the ceiling touch his face ... At one place 'Tige' who is a guard dressed as a dog, suddenly jumps out at him, barking and growling ... Doorways are blockaded so that

guests must crawl through a long dark tunnel ... At the end
he hears a plaintive 'meow' and sees a black cardboard cat out-
lined in luminous paint ... [30]

The guidebook also suggests that different parts of the maze may
have different themes: 'Ghouls Gaol', 'Mad House', 'Tunnel of
Terrors' and 'Dead Man's Gulch' are mentioned. Other tips from
this pre-Second World War guide include a chair wired to deliver
a mild electric shock, the rental of a creepy abandoned house to
hold the event in, and 'Autopsy', in which guests are seated before
a backlit screen behind which fake surgery is performed.

The first haunted houses staged outside of home parties all
seem to have been charitable events, often produced by groups like
the Jaycees (a civic organization dedicated to promoting business
skills among young adults). In the early 1970s, the Christian group
Campus Life staged successful haunted houses across the nation.
These attractions combined many of the techniques of the 'trails
of terror' with heavy amounts of gore and many enthusiastic actors,
and guests typically queued for one to three hours for an experience
that lasted between fifteen and 30 minutes.

Many contemporary 'haunters' – those who create haunted
attractions as a year-round profession – point to one single attraction as the one that most inspired them: the Haunted Mansion at
Disneyland in Anaheim, California. The Mansion opened on 9
August 1969 after more than a decade of planning. It had first been
conceived of as a walk-through attraction, but concerns over moving large masses of guests quickly through the Mansion led to the
use of the 'Omnimover' ride system, small clamshell-shaped cars
that could each pivot 360 degrees, directing the guests' attention to
an exact scene. After Walt Disney died in 1966, the two artists put
in charge of completing the Mansion, long-time 'Imagineers'
Marc Davis and Claude Coats, differed on the artistic direction of
the attraction: Coats felt that guests would want genuine scares,
whereas Davis favoured a lighter, more comedic approach. In the
end, they compromised, with the first half of the ride concentrating
on atmosphere and a few shocks, while the second – set first in a

ballroom, then a cemetery – featured humorous singing ghosts and a knee-rattling caretaker.

What made the Haunted Mansion so successful and so influential, however, was not its similarity to haunted houses and 'dark rides' (that is, tawdry carnival haunted houses) of the past, but its use of startling new technologies and effects. Ghosts were no longer simply sheets hung in a tree, but were instead actual shimmering translucent figures that moved, spoke and sang. A witch wasn't just a rubber-masked figure bent over a fake cauldron, but a completely realistic bodiless head floating in a crystal ball, conducting a complex séance. Projections, the use of 'ghost glass' (which magicians had employed for decades) and pneumatics provided the astonishing effects, and the Mansion also featured intricate sets, beautiful artwork (including paintings that change from tranquil to horrifying), original music and sound effects, and superb voice acting, especially from narrator Paul Frees. The Mansion was an unqualified hit, and soon spawned copies in other Disney theme parks.

But its influence moved well beyond the confines of amusement parks. Edward Douglas, who works with partner Gavin Goszka under the name Midnight Syndicate to create soundtracks for haunted attractions, calls the Haunted Mansion 'the granddaddy of what we do!', and adds that it was 'the very first haunted house that started it all, and certainly the soundtrack that started it all for what we do.'[31] As both domestic and professional haunted houses gained popularity throughout the 1990s and the 2000s, the haunters who had grown up with the Haunted Mansion sought out more advanced technologies for their own Halloween haunts.

One other Southern California amusement park also contributed to the history of haunted attractions: in 1973, Knott's Berry Farm, located near Disneyland in Orange County (about 30 minutes south of Los Angeles) offered one night of Halloween-themed attractions, mainly by adding set dressing and actors to their existing 'Calico Mine Train' ride. The idea proved successful, and the Knott's 'Halloween Haunts' were soon expanded, with most of the 160-acre park being converted for the month of October. In the 1980s, the Halloween events included celebrity stage shows by comedic

Knott's Scary Farm promotional photo, 2000.

performers like 'Weird Al' Yankovic and Elvira. Knott's continued to add mazes and staff to the annual event, and they now boast more than a dozen custom mazes, over 1,000 cast members and state-of-the-art effects and makeup. Knott's employs year-round maze designers who have generated their own followings on websites and Internet message boards. When Knott's debuted a maze based on the film *The Grudge 2* in 2006, it made history not just for its intricate audio-animatronic characters (which included a complete mechanical figure of the film's ghost girl crawling torturously down stairs), but for its cross-marketing campaign, which served to raise awareness of both the film and the maze.

In addition to mazes, 'Knott's Scary Farm', as the Halloween Haunts are also referred to, also employs the use of 'scare zones', large themed outdoor areas through which visitors must pass to reach other parts of the park. In 2011, Knott's featured four scare zones: 'Carnevil', 'Ghost Town', 'Necropolis' and 'Gypsy Camp' (in which werewolves attack a troupe of gypsies). Scare zones have become popular parts of other Halloween theme parks as well.

After Knott's and Disneyland introduced the concept of the major amusement park haunted house, other tourist destinations followed suit. Universal Studios in Orlando introduced 'Fright Nights' in 1991, then in 1992 changed the event's title to the current 'Halloween Horror Nights', which launched at Universal's Hollywood location in 1997. Universal became the first haunted attraction to feature a star celebrity maze designer when they brought horror writer, filmmaker and artist Clive Barker on board in 1998 to design 'Freakz'. Barker eschewed the usual masks purchased from catalogues in favour of custom-designed characters and sets, and went on to design other attractions for Universal in succeeding years. In one interview on his own fascination with Halloween mazes, Barker defined their wide appeal:

> When people come out of the Clive Barker Halloween Maze they've had blood, screaming, madness and monsters. They've survived. There is a sense of, 'I came out the other end of this and I survived.'[32]

Given the success of the seasonal makeovers for existing amusement parks, it was inevitable that an attraction would finally appear that existed only as a Halloween theme park: in 1991, entrepreneur David Bertolino introduced Spookyworld to New England, calling it 'America's Halloween Theme Park'. Although Bertolino sold Spooky World in 2004, in 2010 the park joined with another haunted attraction, Nightmare New England, and continued their tradition of mazes, a 'monster midway' and celebrity appearances by horror film actors and musicians. For several years, Spooky World touted its number one attraction: not a maze or a movie star, but 'Mouse Girl', an actress named Ruth Phelps who let some 200 live mice run over her body while she lay in a large box.

Once the amusement parks had established the notion of the successful seasonal haunted attraction, haunters all over the country followed suit, producing bigger and better attractions every year. By the end of the first decade of the twenty-first century, there was officially a haunted attractions industry that was claiming sales figures of over $6.5 billion a year. Thousands of for-profit haunted houses sprang up all over the country, ranging from simple mazes set up in parking lots to multi-storey adventures that took an hour to walk through. Haunted houses have become the new thrill ride: 'You get the rush without the risk', says David Rudd, dean of the psychology department at Texas Tech. 'As a result, these activities are far more popular than bungee-jumping, sky diving or extreme sports, all of which carry real risks of harm.'[33] Many haunted house entrepreneurs credit not just horror movies or Halloween with the rise in popularity of haunted houses, but also videogames. 'It's like a horror movie, but it's more like a video game. You're moving along in an environment', notes Ben Armstrong, co-owner of Netherworld, a haunted house in Atlanta, Georgia, that plays host to 10,000 guests a night and was voted the nation's top attraction in 2010 by *Haunt-world Magazine*.[34] Netherworld is acclaimed for its use of live actors and makeup effects; other venues, like Philadelphia's Bates Motel (rated #2 by *Hauntworld*) are renowned for their outdoor pyrotech-nics, while some attractions – like The Darkness in St Louis, or 13th Gate in Baton Rouge – are ranked highly for their 'Hollywood quality special effects'.[35] All these attractions provide year-round employment for their owners, and all are housed in permanent loca-tions, usually abandoned factories or warehouses that can be bought or leased cheaply.

Haunted attractions can bring new life to existing neighbour-hoods, but they come with their own specific sets of problems. When the 'Fear City' haunted attraction wanted to set up in Morton Grove, a suburb of northern Chicago, the village board was pleased with the addition of 40 seasonal jobs and the spillover revenue to the local restaurants and gas station, but noise, parking and traffic – con-sidering that an estimated 22,000 people would visit the attraction in less than a month – concerned local residents. The attraction answered many concerns by vowing to hire off-duty police person-nel during the month of October, and Fear City was allowed to take up occupancy in Morton Grove.[36] Apparently Halloween and haunted houses are good for communities feeling the pinch of an economic downturn.

The Piper from the Hallowed Haunting Ground in Studio City, California, 2005.

Another factor contributing to the rise of this relatively new industry was the slow death of physical and makeup effects in Hollywood films as they are replaced with digital effects; the legion of un(der)employed film artists found profitable work in haunted attractions. Dozens if not hundreds of companies work year-round producing full animatronic figures (you can, for example, purchase a chatty Hannibal Lecter robot from Spirit's website for a mere $279.99), body parts, set dressing like cobwebs and headstones, masks and costumes, sound effects, fog effects and set pieces such as inflatable maze walls. These companies display their wares every year at Transworld, the industry's trade show; there are also websites, print magazines, how-to videos and books on this burgeoning and lucrative new staple of Halloween.

The haunted attractions industry, however, doesn't cater only to the professional; it also sells to home haunters who might stage a small maze in their front yard, or simply decorate the yard in an extravagant fashion (known in the industry lingo as a 'soft yard haunt'). Some of the earliest home haunts to achieve fame beyond their neighbourhood were set in Los Angeles, where access to Hollywood special effects experts or original props and set pieces could be had more easily. One of the best known of the early haunters was Bob Burns, a memorabilia collector who every Halloween turned his San Fernando Valley home into a recreation of a different classic horror or science fiction film; his haunts were so effective that Burns received both local and national news coverage. In 1976, when Burns re-created the 1960 film *The Time Machine* in his yard, he used the original machine and was even visited by the film's producer George Pal. His recreation of *Alien* in 1979 (the same year the film was released) featured *Star Trek* actor Walter Koenig as the doomed starship captain. Burns's last show, in 2002, was a detailed rendition of Howard Hawks's *The Thing From Another World* (1951).

The influence of Disneyland's Haunted Mansion was to be found in another famous Southern California home haunt, the Hallowed Haunting Grounds in Studio City. The haunt, which ran until 2005 and has been featured in haunted attraction magazines, websites and videos, literally recreated some of the Mansion's effects in a typical suburban front yard, offering views of floating lanterns, a bodiless talking medium and translucent ghosts. The Hallowed Haunting Grounds drew approximately 3,000 visitors a year.

By the time some of the home haunt pioneers were retiring, commercially produced effects were becoming cheaper and more readily available to casual Halloween decorators. It didn't matter any longer if you weren't in the Hollywood area with access to special effects knowhow; by the 2000s, $1,699 would buy a marble grave sculpture that would abruptly transform into a jabbering ghoul, all set in motion by sensors. Some home haunters, like Eric Lowther of Exeter, New Hampshire, started staging displays so popular that the street had to be blocked off to cope with the thousands of visitors. Lowther eventually moved his display to a farm, and now uses his haunt to raise money for charity.

One of the oddest off-shoots of both the haunted attractions industry and Christianity's love/hate relationship with Halloween is the 'Hell House'. This kind of Christian-themed haunted event presents a series of moralistic tableaux under the guise of a traditional Halloween walk-through attraction; however, guests don't truly interact with the scenes, as they do in a typical haunted house, but are rather passive audience members for a series of short plays that each present the commission of a sin (in a gruesome fashion). The last room in a Hell House usually involves a prayer meeting with the pastor or minister in which he attempts to convert the paying guests to his church. Hell houses may have first appeared in the 1970s, but they didn't attract major attention until a Colorado pastor named Keenan Roberts began selling a 'Hell House Outreach' kit. Priced at $299, the kit includes instructions on how to run a Hell House; for additional fees, Hell House presenters can also purchase optional extra scenes that include 'Gay Wedding', 'Post-birth Abortion' and 'Cyber-chick Multimedia' (the last offers 'contemporary TNT to caution of the dangerous cesspool the Internet can become'[37]). There are now hundreds of Hell Houses offered in the United States every year, and they claim a 35 per cent conversion rate.

Growing alongside the haunted attractions industry is the Halloween attractions industry, which focuses not on adult hauntings but on family-friendly and agriculturally themed seasonal festivities, including corn mazes and pumpkin patches. Since haunted houses – with their high levels of gore effects and intense shocks – are unsuitable for small children, the Halloween attraction business is filling that gap for the young ones. Sometimes referred to as 'agri-tourism' or 'agri-tainment', corn mazes and pumpkin patches not only provide families with a kid-friendly, old-fashioned autumn/Halloween experience, but have proven an economic boon for farmers. Corn mazes, which can occupy anywhere from two acres to more than 40, can produce as much as 200 times the profit that the same land would generate by simply being used for growing and harvesting corn. Corn mazes probably grew out of the long tradition of hedge mazes in Europe, but recent advances in GPS technology have given rise to dozens of professional maze planning and designing companies. A corn maze is always cut in a complicated design, which could be anything from the farm's logo to a state flag, and is created from special hybrid corn; visitors pay a fee to enter and are provided with maps. Corn mazes and pumpkin patches usually form the heart of a Halloween experience that might also include face-painting, crafts and foods displays, contests, playgrounds and hayrides. Sometimes corn mazes are transformed in the evening into haunted attractions, with monsters stationed throughout the maze.

Pumpkin patches and pumpkin growing have also benefited from recent new advances. Farmers in the eastern part of the U.S. grow special hybrid pumpkins in hopes of winning the prize for the largest pumpkin of the year; so far, achieving a one-ton pumpkin has remained an elusive goal, although recent prize-winners have come within nearly 200 pounds. Specially grown oversized pumpkins have also been turned into boats for events such as Nova Scotia's Windsor Pumpkin Regatta, in which immense, hollowed-out pumpkins are rowed or motored for specified distances.

Technology continues to move forward, and the haunt industry moves with it. Aside from increasingly amazing and affordable robotics, there are now 3D technologies that equip maze customers with glasses and offer them a walk-through 3D experience, usually assisted by the liberal use of fluorescent paints and black lights;

Pumpkin patch at Forneris Farms in Mission Hills, California.

motion sensors and infrared cameras that detect the presence of guests and activate a scare; plasma television screens that play back an excessively horrifying scene with more realism than can be achieved with a robot; zip-lines that can allow actors to pass overhead; and 'slider gloves' that, when raked along an asphalt surface, produce showers of phosphorescent sparks.

Twenty-first Century Halloween Tricks

Advanced technologies, however, have also produced a few less pleasant Halloween scares in the new millennium. Urban legends – once limited to what could be reported in papers or passed via word of mouth – are now spread on 4G networks almost at the speed of thought. The 9/11 terrorist attack on the United States in 2001 didn't dampen the spirits of trick or treaters the way many experts had predicted it would (although policeman and firefighter costumes were more popular that year), but it did spawn several new urban legends, including one involving anthrax-laced candy and one in which 'my friend's friend was dating a guy from Afghanistan' who warned her not to board any planes on either 9/11 or Halloween.[38] A legend that's been passed around since the mid-1980s is that of the haunted house that's either impossible to survive or will offer money back to patrons who make it all the way through. In 2008, a man named Andrew T. Lazaro was actually arrested for spreading malicious Halloween rumours on the Internet, all of which centred on a supposed gang initiation in which new members would shoot schoolgirls and women on Halloween night. The search to find Lazaro – who made the postings on 30 October, but wasn't arrested until 1 December – intensified after schools brought in extra security and cancelled certain events.

Costuming has also ventured down some questionable new avenues in recent years. Dressing pets in costumes was one thing – the American Pet Products Association reported that Halloween costumes were one of the top trends in pet retailing for 2011[39] – but putting Fido or Kitty in a pirate outfit for Halloween was nothing in comparison to what was happening in human costuming. The second half of the 2000s saw an explosion in the sales of sexually provocative Halloween costumes, especially those aimed at women; everything from traditional hoboes and clowns to Disney heroines to the Tim Burton character 'Edward Scissorhands' could now be had in a 'sexy' version for women. Sociologists, psychologists and feminists debated the positives and negatives of this trend, some decrying the 'hypersexualization' while others applauded the costumes as 'empowering'. Dr Deborah Tolman, director of the Center for Research on Gender and Sexuality at San Francisco State University, suggested that these costumes might be a way for women to mock the overly sexualized images of women presented in advertising and media: 'Hey, if we can claim Halloween as a safe space to question these images being sold to us, I think that's a great idea.'[40] However, child psychologists worried about the effect on girls, since sexy costumes (like 'French Maid') were now marketed to children as young as eight years old. 'Studies show that the oversexualization of girls correlates with depression and eating disorders', noted psychiatrist Dr Gail Saltz in a discussion of Halloween costumes for teens and younger children.[41] Schools began to ban Halloween costumes and parties because girls were dressing too provocatively and boys were using too many violence-themed accessories such as fake weapons.

One group has even called for an end to costumes that promote stereotypes of mental illness: in 2002, the National Alliance on Mental Illness (NAMI) protested against the selling of costumes like 'the Straight Jacket' and the use in haunted attractions of scenes involving electroshock therapy or insane asylums. NAMI's executive director Rick Birkel noted:

> Halloween costumes portraying hospital patients in straitjackets, or haunted houses presented as insane asylums, are no different than the blackface minstrel shows in an earlier era, when African Americans were cruelly caricatured, segregated and marginalized in our society.[42]

The group was successful in getting the Pepsi company, which was sponsoring the Atlanta haunted attraction Netherworld and its 'Inner Sanctum' theme, to remove its logo from Netherworld's website; however, Spencer Gifts, parent company to the Spirit Halloween stores, stated that they would continue to 'poke fun at life situations whenever and wherever we find them'.[43]

Fundamentalist Christians groups continue to call for the abolishment of anything they deem pagan or Satanic, and have published literally hundreds of cautionary books and web pages which often begin by quoting Vallancey and then descend to even more fantastic depths. Writing about how Samhain was practiced by the ancient Celts, one book notes, 'As part of the celebration, people donned grotesque masks and danced around the great bonfires often pretending they were being pursued by evil spirits', while the jack-o'-lantern 'may have originated with the witches' use of a skull with a candle in it to light the way to coven meetings.'[44] In 2009, even the Vatican weighed in, running an article in its newspaper, *L'Osservatore Romano*, entitled 'Halloween's Dangerous Messages'. The author of the article, Joan Maria Canals, stated: 'Halloween has an undercurrent of occultism and is absolutely anti-Christian.' He suggested that parents should 'try to direct the meaning of the feast towards wholesomeness and beauty rather than terror, fear and death'.[45] (After this story received considerable negative reactions, many clerics pointed out that the Vatican had issued no official statement on Halloween, and that its newspaper was run by an independent editorial board.[46]) Some reverends, among others, have countered by suggesting that if Christians are to ban celebrations on the basis of their pagan origins, they might want to start with Christmas and Easter.

Religious concerns over Halloween have also spread to schools. In Northern California, high schools banned Halloween celebrations because of fears that they violated the constitutional right to freedom of religion. 'Teaching about Halloween will fall under the guidelines of teaching about religious beliefs and customs', Los Altos school board president Phil Faillace said. 'And school time may not be used to celebrate Halloween, just as it may not be used to celebrate Easter, Yom Kippur or Ramadan.'[47]

Schools and churches weren't the only ones who were mistrustful of Halloween by the 1990s. Around 1992, lists of common phobias began to include 'samhainophobia', a fear of Halloween. Dozens of websites now exist purporting to be skilled in treating this condition – which may be accompanied by or related to other phobias, including placophobia, a fear of tombstones or burial, or ailurophobia, fear of cats – even though there are virtually no documented cases of it.

Employers and parents have had their own reasons to dread Halloween. By 2010, one in three Americans planned to either hold or attend a Halloween party, with many parents preferring to stage parties for their teenagers and friends rather than risk letting the adolescents engage in unsafe behaviour on the night. Most parents spend considerable time and money decorating or preparing costumes for their children, and companies worry about employee costuming – inappropriate costumes, including those that are overtly sexual or portray offensive stereotypes, can be disruptive. American employers 'are likely to see an uptick in absences' around Halloween, according to one workforce-management company.[48] Employees are taking more time off for Halloween, and yet 25 per cent of American households each year are still expected to run out of candy for trick or treaters.

New studies on Halloween – and surely the fact that Halloween is now the subject of studies proves how thoroughly accepted into mass culture it has become – have indicated other reasons for stress as well. A Yale University study found that birth rates actually decreased on Halloween (as compared to Valentine's Day, when they rose), while an article in *Psychology Today* called Halloween 'the new New Year's' in terms of the social pressures experienced by young adults anxious to connect and network.[49] To modern urbanites, Halloween's fears are more about social pressures than malevolent sprites and the coming winter.

In the twenty-first century, Halloween has survived terrorist attacks, economic downturns, malicious urban legends and increasingly terrifying haunted attractions only to become bigger than ever. Contrary to dour predictions, costumed American tots are still demanding candy on the evening of 31 October, but adults now have the option of participating in trick or treat or heading out to enjoy an evening of carefully staged (and sexy) scares. Folklorist and Halloween expert Jack Santino has summed it up this way:

Halloween in the u.s., then, has been changing and adapting for over a century. Before World War ii it was celebrated with parties in the home; it then became a masked solicitation ritual, and is now an inversive, large-scale public festival.[50]

Now, as the twenty-first century enters its second decade, Halloween is becoming something else: the latest mega-successful American export to tantalize happy consumers around the globe.

4

La Toussaint, Allerheiligen and *Tutti i Santi*: The Global Celebration

Halloween has become popular throughout almost the entire English-speaking world: from Ireland, where Samhain combines with All Saints' Day, to Great Britain and finally to North America, where the day has its most fervent fans, Halloween has spread down through two millennia. It's also found favour in Canada, where trick or treat may have been born, and more isolated areas like the Isle of Man. The festival has received a mixed reception throughout the rest of the world, however. American expatriates around the globe have often brought Halloween with them, although in the past it was limited to little more than home parties or events at nightclubs. But over the last ten years, a combination of American media – especially seasonal films like *Halloween* and *The Nightmare Before Christmas*, and Halloween-themed episodes of American television series – merchandising from large global chains like McDonald's, and theme parks looking for revenue during the slow autumn season have created a new wave of global interest in Halloween. Halloween's appeal for children, especially costuming and trick or treat, have made the holiday far more commercially successful than other festivals (such as Valentine's Day) that are focused more on adults. As one folklorist has noted, 'Halloween builds on an unbeatable combination of terror, children and sweets, and comes slap bang in the middle of an otherwise boring and ever darkening autumnal season.'[1]

In most of Continental Europe, the American Halloween is just starting to gain in popularity – or has already peaked and is

Four West Yorkshire revellers celebrate Halloween with sparklers.

now waning again – but there is already a longstanding tradition of celebrating 1 November with visits to graveyards in observance of All Saints' and All Souls' Days. In areas where the Catholic religion remains predominant, 1 November may also involve church attendance (All Saints' is a holy day of obligation in the Catholic Church, and up until 1955 was celebrated with an octave, or eight-day-long period of prayer following the actual day) and hearing of special masses commemorating the dead. In contrast to Ireland's pranking, Scotland's fortune-telling and America's treat-begging, the end of October and beginning of November in Europe was, until the recent introduction of Halloween, a quiet time with an emphasis on remembering deceased loved ones. Interestingly, in many areas of Europe, Halloween seems to be regarded as completely distinct from All Saints' Day, even unrelated.

The notion that Halloween is really little more than Samhain renamed has become pervasive in popular culture; books, articles and websites have all routinely ascribed everything from bonfires and pranking to trick or treat to the ancient Celts. A website on Halloween history, for example, states that costuming came about when the Celts 'dressed as ghouls to fool evil spirits let loose on

October 31'.[2] The official website for Sweden goes even further, ascribing not just costuming and trick or treat to Samhain, but also jack-o'-lantern carving.[3] The Dutch have even tried to claim Halloween's identity by rewriting history and suggesting that 'the Celts already celebrated Halloween in the Netherlands'.[4] The late Austrian folklorist Editha Hörnander saw the use of references to a Celtic past as Halloween was imported into Europe as a kind of label used by the media which provided consumers with a (false) sense of historical continuity and a connection to a distant past.[5] This 'branding' could help to explain why Halloween (a pagan celebration) has been viewed in Europe as – despite the meaning of its name – completely separate from the Christian festivals of All Saints and All Souls.

Culture Clash in Europe

The region of Europe in which 1 and 2 November most closely resemble the English-speaking Halloween prior to its arrival in America is Brittany, the large peninsula to the northwest of France. This is not entirely surprising, since Brittany is considered (along with Cornwall, Ireland, Scotland, Wales and the Isle of Man) to be one of the six Celtic Nations. Breton, still spoken throughout much of the area, is a Celtic language that shares its origin with the Welsh and Cornish tongues, and although the folklore of the region contains no references to Samhain – celebration that was probably confined to the Irish Celts – there is none the less a wealth of eerie, ghostly beliefs centred on All Saints' and (especially) All Souls' Days. Around 1900, travel authors were still referring to Brittany as 'medieval', and the Bretons believed that the dead returned on *Le Jour des morts*. Fishermen at sea on All Souls' Eve risked having their boats invaded by the spirits of those who had drowned, now seeking passage back to land for a proper burial. Those on shore this evening might hear the voices of loved ones who had drowned, begging for prayers to be said in their names. In the Carnac area of Brittany, peasants . . . believe that on the night of All Souls' the church is lighted by supernatural means, and in the graveyard the graves give forth the dead, who wend their way along the road, to a church, where Death in the pulpit preaches a wordless, soundless sermon to a vast gathering of kneeling skeletons.[6]

Throughout most of Brittany, All Saints' Day was for sombre remembrance of the dead, who were thought to return at midnight. During the day families prayed in church, where 'Black Vespers' (prayers made around a catafalque draped in black) were observed as per the Catholic Roman Rite. After the service, the entire parish then visited graveyards, where the priest blessed the graves. In the evenings, they placed food and drink – traditional pancakes and cider – out for deceased loved ones, and fires were left burning in hearths so the dead could warm themselves (these were built around the *kef-am-Anaon*, or 'the Log of the Dead'). Bretons retired early on All Saints' Eve, and avoided leaving home, since the roads were filled with wandering spirits; however, if it was absolutely necessary to venture outside, any small work tool, even a thimble or a needle, carried in a pocket would provide protection against malicious spirits.

Graveyards were an important feature of life in old Brittany, and many featured *lanternes des mort*; these curious structures were tall (seven to ten meters) stone towers surmounted by a lantern. They were often built in French cemeteries during the twelfth to fourteenth centuries. In Brittany, the lanterns were kept burning throughout the night on All Souls' Eve.

A classic Breton cautionary tale tells of Wilherm (or Yann) Postik, a true son of *an eol kornek* (the horned angel). Wilherm refused to attend church, and didn't mourn when his mother, sister and wife all passed away. On All Souls' Eve, a drunken Wilherm unwisely took a shortcut known to be a road of the dead, and soon encountered a large black carriage driven by the *Ankou*, the Breton equivalent of the Grim Reaper. Wilherm escaped the *Ankou* but then met washerwomen wringing out a winding sheet; he recognized among them his dead mother, sister and wife. Before he could respond, he was wound in the sheet, and the next morning he was found dead. When consecrated candles wouldn't burn near him, those who found him knew he had been damned.

Music also figured prominently in Breton observances. A lengthy *gwerz*, or hymn, was sung in the graveyard during the day and at night 'The Death Singers' moved among the houses, imploring sleepers to arise and pray for the dead.

Beyond Brittany, France has celebrated *La Toussaint* with graveyard visits on 1 November, but Halloween as a 31 October celebration has never found widespread acceptance there. It is estimated that between 83 and 88 per cent of French people are Catholics and All Saints' Day in France retains much of its Catholic character, being traditionally celebrated with visits to cemeteries and decoration of graves.[7] Chrysanthemums are the flowers of choice – in fact, such is their association with *La Toussaint* that they are not given as gifts throughout the rest of the year – and traffic routes around cemeteries are clogged to capacity on the day, a public holiday throughout France. Popular cemeteries such as Père Lachaise in Paris are said to draw tens of thousands of visitors.

All Saints' Day turned political in Montmartre on 2 November 1868. Thousands poured into the cemetery that day to search for the tomb of Alphonse Baudin, a representative of the people who had died seventeen years earlier. Baudin's tomb had been reported lost for seventeen years, but anger against the Imperial government was at its highest and the searchers finally located the gravesite. After covering the tomb with *immortelles* and using it as a platform from which to deliver fiery revolutionary speeches, some of the visitors clashed with police. The event led a few liberal papers to call for a memorial to Baudin, which resulted in government fines being levied on their editors.

One of the oddest French references to Halloween can be found in a story from 1836 by Honoré de Balzac, 'The Story of the Lidless Eye'. The piece is essentially a parody of Burns, and is set in 'Cassilis' – no doubt a direct reference to the Burns poems, which begins with a reference to Cassilis Downans – on Halloween. Balzac is in error regarding many of the most basic facts of Halloween, and it's difficult to know if he was simply unaware of it and its relation to *La Toussaint*, or if he was deliberately poking fun at Burns. 'Doubtless, you do not know what Hallowe'en is', begins one paragraph near the beginning of the story, 'it is the night of the fairies; it occurs about the middle of August.' Balzac goes on to refer to Sir Walter Scott as 'a Scottish peasant', and describes the wild Halloween revels of 'boglilles', 'brownlilles' and 'spunkies'.[8]

In the mid-1980s, Halloween first began to make some small inroads into French culture and, a decade later, companies like McDonald's were using Halloween-themed advertising campaigns in France. Disneyland Paris redecorated its Main Street attraction as 'Spook Street', pumpkins appeared in markets, and bakers and chocolatiers offered seasonal sweets. In 1996, the town of Limoges inaugurated a parade which drew 30,000 people, and also held numerous costume parties and contests.

However, all that began to change by 2002. In a country frequently described as being 'keen to protect itself from what it sees as u.s. cultural dominance',[9] Halloween – which arrived in France largely on the backs of American businesses like Disney and McDonald's – proved a relatively unsuccessful import. Halloween retailing in France declined sharply in the twenty-first century, and by 2006 the festival was declared dead in France. The newspapers *Le Monde* and *Le Parisien* reported that Halloween in France had already been 'pretty much buried', and in reporting this declaration, Forbes. com cited 'falling sales and anti-Americanism' as the chief reasons for its failure.[10]

Halloween has received a much warmer reception in Belgium, however. *Aller-Heiligen Dag*, or All Saints' Day, has been observed there with grave visiting and candle lighting, and All Souls' was celebrated with the eating of special cakes in the belief that each cake eaten marked another soul rescued from Purgatory. Poor children were said to place tables before their houses with pictures of the Madonna featured thereon in order to beg the cakes from passers-by.

Early twentieth-century visitors to Belgium reported that the country had its own set of spooky All Saints' Day myths:

Belgian peasants say that on the Eve of All Souls unquiet spirits are loosed from their graves for an hour after sunset. Those who died by violence, or those who died unshriven, rise from the dark and speak to passersby; with the load of their sins upon them, with the hatred, or fear, or agony, or longing which they felt while dying, still in their tortured hearts, they beg the passersby to take vengeance on their enemies, or to give them news of those they loved or hated. And after a brief hour they sink back again into the dust.[11]

Over the last three years, Halloween's importation into Belgium has begun to thrive, with even isolated villages now engaging in trick or treat – although in some villages the practice seems to be occurring in the weeks before and after Halloween, as well as on the actual night itself. Halloween's popularity in Belgium has also gained a considerable boost from the popular amusement park Walibi Belgium, located near Brussels. In 2007, Walibi Belgium introduced 'Fright Nights', and almost immediately drew record crowds; the park converted its usual attractions to Halloween themes, and added mazes and scare zones. One difference between Walibi's haunted attractions and its American cousins seems to be in the way the actors interact with guests: apparently Walibi's monsters have no personal space issues, and will frequently touch guests or back them into tight corners and refuse to allow them to leave.

In northern European countries, Halloween has recently caught on thanks to the usual combination of retailing, theme parks, and movies and television, but it's also enjoyed – as is noted on the official website for Sweden – as 'a welcome diversion in the gathering dark'.[12] These countries still celebrate both All Saints' Day (with lighting of graves in the evening) and Martinmas (in the Netherlands, children still beg house-to-house on Martinmas, even though trick or treat takes place only eleven days earlier). The Church of Sweden has even used Halloween as a way to further promote All Saints' Day by teaching Halloween-hungry children about the day after.

The appeal of pumpkins, with their bright orange, easy-to-carve rind and late autumn ripening, seems to be almost universal, and has provided the basis for some of the Halloween festivities now appearing in the Scandinavian countries. The Swedish island of Öland, for example, has turned Halloween pumpkin growing into an important part of its economy, and now holds a *Skördefesten* or harvest festival towards the end of every September, complete with a *pumpagubbe* or pumpkin man (a large harvest figure with a pumpkin head). The summer sun in Sweden shines for eighteen hours a day, which is ideal for sun-loving pumpkin crops. Forty varieties, including giant pumpkins used only in contests, are grown on Öland; pumpkins are rotated with other crops and fertilized with mulch from local livestock, since Swedish farmers pride themselves on organic practices.

In Denmark, the famed amusement park Tivoli Gardens has created a mid-October Halloween celebration that has been drawing record crowds since 2006 and boasts a display of more than 15,000 pumpkins as well as 'the biggest pumpkin in Denmark'. 'Halloween in Tivoli' is slanted towards family entertainment, with a harvest celebration and activities for children. Interestingly, Halloween in Denmark is celebrated a week before 31 October, probably to coincide with a pre-existing autumn school break.

In Germany, where less than a quarter of the population is Roman Catholic, All Saints' and All Souls' Days have been celebrated, but Halloween is now finding a warmer reception there. All Saints' Day, or *Allerheiligen*, was observed with the lighting of special candles called *Seelenlichter* that were left burning throughout the night. All Souls' Day, or *Allerseelen*, was the start of an eight-day period called *Seelennächte* or 'Soul Nights', a time for performing acts of charity or penance. Special cakes – *Seelenbrot* or *Allerheiligenstrieze* – are still given out; these sweet breads are made from plaited strands of dough and may be sprinkled with poppy seeds. A number of superstitions were traditionally associated with *Allerseelen*: hot pans or upturned blades weren't left out during the evening, for fear that wandering spirits would injure themselves; bowls of fat or butter were made available to soothe the wounds of the dead.

Walking three times around a church on this evening would guarantee that a wish would come true, and a girl might leave the house on this night and ask the name of the first man she encountered, since that would be the name of her future husband.

All Saints' Day was traditionally celebrated with graveyard visits, although the Germans at one time hired mourners for graves they couldn't visit. This description from Munich in 1892 suggests this practice wasn't always viewed favourably:

> On the morning of All Saints' Day the families greet each other over the resting-places of those they loved, arranging, adorning, and praying in faithful hope, or weeping in sad remembrance. There are but few signs of mourning to be seen. Light and life reign everywhere; the loveliest flowers and

Trick-or-treaters in Sweden.

plants bloom on the graves; cypresses and weeping-willows wave and rustle in the breeze; and if anything reminds us of the chilliness of death or the gloom that we dread, it is the lifeless forms of the hired male and female grave-watchers, who stand near the mounds to tend the lamps and flowers, mechanically repeating their rosary, contemplating sullenly and indifferently the imposing spectacle around them, and longing for the evening, when the reward which has been promised them is to be paid. In the evening these repugnant figures leave the garden, but they take away with them the flowers and lights, and the feast is at an end.[13]

The more Americanized celebration of Halloween is a relatively recent arrival, and may have begun in earnest in 1975, when an American soldier named Brian Hill organized a Halloween party, broadcast the news over the American Forces Network and drew 5,000 revellers. The event was held at Castle Frankenstein, an actual ruined fortress dating back a thousand years, located a short distance south of Darmstadt. The success of that first celebration led to an annual party. In 1991, the event was scaled back for fear of damaging the ruins and was extended over three weekends to accommodate and spread out visitors. Castle Frankenstein's Halloween is still held, hosts around 15,000 visitors annually and offers shows, themed areas, special times for children and 80 costumed actors.

Halloween has also been introduced into Germany via television and films, theme parks and retailing. Although films such as John Carpenter's *Halloween* and Tim Burton's *The Nightmare Before Christmas* have been popular there, the biggest boost to Halloween has been the importation of American episodic television in which Halloween celebrations are commonly featured. As of 2009, Halloween had 'become part of the cultural capital (and hence of the identity) of a generation of young Germans'.[14]

Germany is one of only two countries that celebrate another 31 October celebration: Reformation Day, in memory of Martin Luther's presentation in 1517 of his 'Ninety-Five Theses', which began the Protestant Reformation. In Germany, only five states recognize Reformation Day as a public holiday; however, in Slovenia, the day is a national holiday. By way of contrast, Slovenia – where All Saints' Day is also a public holiday – has been reluctant to embrace Halloween. Although most Slovenian media have suggested that Halloween is held in contempt there mainly because of anti-American sentiments, the country also seems unwilling to risk replacing its celebration of Reformation Day.

Halloween still has yet to make much of an inroad into Eastern Europe, due partly to deeply ingrained All Saints' Day observances, but also owing to some other unexpected cultural factors. Pumpkins, for instance: while the happy orange squash has helped spread Halloween through other areas of Europe, pumpkins already had their own special meaning in Ukraine, where they traditionally symbolized a woman's rejection of a suitor. Even though this tradition has faded, the pumpkin – or *harbuz* in Ukrainian – retains a negative connotation in Eastern Europe; a business deal might be turned down by saying, 'I have to hand you a pumpkin on that one.'[15]

All Saints' Day – or *Dzień Wszystkich Świętych* – is a national holiday in Poland, where the number of travellers visiting cemeteries leads each year to an increase in car accidents on 1 November. Local stores sell special headstone-cleaning solutions and at the graveside Poles light special candles called *znicz*. Radio broadcasts feature the work of late musical artists, and Polish writers and artists also use the day to raise money to restore and remember old monuments and graves. Many Poles also visit the grounds of the notorious Nazi concentration camp Auschwitz 1 on 1 November, remembering Polish prisoners who died there by placing flowers and candles at graves and even on the train tracks leading into the camp.

Some have suggested that the Polish reverence for All Saints' Day has made them slow to embrace Halloween. Indeed, American teachers who have attempted to tell schoolchildren about it have found angry parents removing their children from the classroom with an exclamation of, 'We do not celebrate such a holiday.'[16] Historian Allen Paul has suggested that Halloween's aura of rowdy indulgence can't compete with the fierce nationalism generated by Poland's All Saints' Day traditions, since Polish lives lost to the invasions of the Second World War and the long struggles under communism are commemorated on this day.[17]

One Eastern European country, however, has definitely claimed part of Halloween for itself: Romania, home to Transylvania. The popularity of bats as Halloween icons isn't the only gift that Bram Stoker's *Dracula* has given to Halloween: the novel forever transformed the province of Transylvania into the metaphorical capital of all things supernatural, and Romanian locals have embraced the story of the vampire count along with the tourism dollars it has provided. Halloween tours to Transylvania now typically include visits to the Borgo Pass, where the novel's opening is set; Bran Castle, now dubbed Dracula's Castle; and Sighisoara, the birthplace of Vlad Tepes, the fifteenth-century Wallachian prince known as 'Vlad the Impaler', whose name, Dracula – meaning 'Son of the Dragon' – inspired Stoker in the creation of his vampire.

In Spain, *Dia de Todos los Santos* (All Saints' Day) has been observed with the same traditions found in most other Catholic areas of Europe: families visit churches in the morning and then proceed to cemeteries, where they clean and decorate the graves of loved ones. Often they use expensive black-painted brass lamps, which are first lit during the day on 1 November and left burning until the end of the festival. Travel guides in the nineteenth century suggested that All Saints' Day cemetery visits were less of a religious observance, however, and more of a 'fashionable promenade', thronged with vendors and beggars.[18] The festival was kept for three days, during which time most shops were closed to allow daily visits to the graveyards.

All Saints' Day in Catalonia was until recently a fairly minor festival, celebrated mainly through seasonal foods: chestnuts, sweet potatoes and a special cake called *panellet*. Although Spanish immigrants brought some other traditions with them, chiefly the visiting of graves on All Saints' Day, much of Catalonia is secular, and 31 October served more as a recognition of autumn. However, Halloween – distinctly different from the more sombre celebration of All Saints' Day – has begun to grow in popularity there, disseminated via retailing and schools. Catalonian sociologist Salvador

Cardús has suggested that Halloween's popularity has grown with the number and diversity of immigrants, including many Muslims: 'Halloween has arrived in our country completely secularized, as a simple celebration of disguises to give you a fright.'[19]

In many areas of northern Spain, the American ritual of trick or treat has been accepted, and costumed children can now be found parading through the streets on Halloween night. There is one difference between this Spanish trick or treat and its American cousin, however: in Spain, the children visit only shops and restaurants, not private homes.

A popular Catalan sitcom called *Plats Bruts*, first aired from 1999 to 2002, ran an episode entitled '*Tinc Castanyes*' ('I've Got Chestnuts') which addressed the clash between traditional All Saints' Day observances in Catalonia and Western-style Halloween.[20] In the episode, Lopez, a traditional Catalan who is shown preparing *panellets* for the festival, confronts David, a roommate who is more interested in modern celebrations and who is shown in Halloween costume as a vampire and carving a pumpkin. Lopez complains that the American celebration is 'imperialist', but his insistence on celebrating in traditional ways is also mocked.

Italy – which, as the home of the Vatican and the birthplace of All Saints' Day could certainly be considered the original home of Halloween, as much as Celtic Ireland – has had a long romance with All Saints' (*Ognissanti* or *Tutti i Santi*) and All Souls' Day, (*Il Giorno dei Morti*), and is just starting to welcome Halloween into the fold. The Pantheon in Rome, which served to inaugurate All Saints' Day in AD 609, still holds special masses for All Saints' Day, which include an orchestra. Visiting cemeteries is practiced on both 1 and 2 November, and has a long – and sometimes strange – history in Italy. In 1888, the *Saturday Review* described All Saints' Day activities in Naples, and complained that the graveyard visits 'degenerate into a pleasure-party', with visitors maintaining 'a decent sobriety' on the way to the cemeteries, but stopping at the numerous inns lining the roads on the way back. This same article describes a church in Ravello that celebrated All Souls' by placing 'a disgusting effigy ... in the court dress of some former century' before the altar.[21] The author admits that he didn't pause to inquire whether this object was an actual mummy or merely a realistic mannequin.

Some nineteenth-century Italian churches, including La Morte and Santa Maria in Trastevere, were famed for presenting theatrical re-enactments of scenes from the lives of the saints on All Saints' Day, with the various participants represented by realistic wax figures. In 1868, the cemetery of San Giovanni offered a plague scene featuring the holy man Camillo de Lellis surrounded by 'Groups of plague-stricken people ... women gasping, children in dying agony, men whose faces were covered with purple spots and who were foaming at the mouth.'[22] But nothing surpassed the realism of a scene presented in the cemetery of the San Spirito Hospital in 1823, when the corpses of those who had recently passed away in the hospital were arrayed in a ring around the waxen figure of an angel with its horn pointed toward heaven. It's hard to imagine even the most sophisticated twenty-first century haunted attraction surpassing that for sheer shock effect.

As in Brittany and other areas, it was popular to leave food out for visiting spirits on All Saints' or All Souls' Eve. In Salerno, until the fifteenth century it was customary to leave a large meal out for the dead before the family departed for church; it was believed that any food left over foretold ill fortune. Apparently – and unsurprisingly – this ritual drew large numbers of thieves to the city.

One of the most interesting seasonal foods found in Italy is *fave dei morti*, a sweet made of sugar and almonds and intended to represent beans – the same beans, no doubt, that were strewn around the household to drive out spirits on the final evening of the ancient Roman festival of Lemuria. The final night of Lemuria took place on 13 May, the original date assigned to All Saints' Day.

Food was also begged on the evening of 1 November, but not by children; instead, parish priests went house-to-house, asking for small gifts of food which they shared among themselves throughout that night. Children, however, did figure prominently in one belief from Sicily: on the evening of 1 November, it was believed that the souls of the dead would rise, return to their homes and fill the stockings of good tots with toys and sweets. The little ones were

'Carnevale', from *Rome ancienne et moderne* (Paris, 1865).

warned not to try to stay awake to view the dead in action; to do so would ensure no rewards, but the children might find themselves touched or tickled by the cold fingers of the spirits.

Fave dei morti are still made and eaten throughout Italy on 1 November, but cemetery visits are reported to be on the decline. Halloween, however, is finding a home in Italy, much in the same way it has throughout the rest of Europe. Halloween is sometimes referred to as '*la notte delle streghe*' ('night of the witches') in Italy, and both pumpkins and trick or treat have become increasingly popular. In cities like Venice, where elaborate costuming has a long tradition, Halloween is reportedly catching up to Carnevale in terms of the size of the celebrations. Some cities in Italy have also become popular tourist destinations on Halloween: Palermo, for example, is visited for its Capuchin Catacombs, which house 8,000 mummies.

The Russian Debate

Halloween has found an uneasy home in Russia, where its popularity has burgeoned since the 1990s despite fears from some vocal Russians that it has blossomed while traditional home-grown celebrations have been allowed to fade away. Halloween seems to have first been introduced in Russia by American teachers of English, who soon found that it was a favourite with their students. One teacher even used Halloween to stage a mock hanging of the class dunce, an event which understandably drew some parental fire. In 2003, the Moscow Department of Education issued a statement condemning the practice of Halloween activities in schools. However, schools were split over whether to follow the suggestion or continue to celebrate the day. In a interview of 2006, Russian Orthodox priest Mikhail Prokopenko attacked Halloween on both nationalist and religious fronts: 'The celebration of Halloween in Russia has become quite popular. This fact shows that we should be more careful with borrowing foreign holidays', Father Prokopenko noted, before adding, 'a young man or a woman, who dress like vampires or demons, are led to believe that they can display monsters' qualities in real life',[23] surely one of the oddest criticisms of Halloween on record.

Despite disapproval from both government and religion, by 2010, Halloween in Russia was said to be 'growing exponentially'.[24] Halloween remains especially popular with young adults, and events held at nightclubs on 31 October usually sell out. Some clubs have attempted to 'Russify' Halloween by urging patrons to wear Russian-themed costumes and by providing traditional Russian foods and beverages. However, most patrons prefer something more traditional to the American-style Halloween, and vampires, witches and zombies are all on view.

Halloween may be catching on in Russia becuase it is viewed as a way of expressing art on a personal level. The Moscow School of Body Art, for example, encourages students to participate in the festival and to consider its potential as a lucrative part of their careers. As one of the school's makeup artists explained, 'From the beginning,

Halloween was more than just a holiday. It's encouraging people to make costumes themselves. It's a kind of art, which is great.'[25]

Decadence in the Middle East

Technically, Halloween shouldn't be found in the Middle East: those of the Jewish, Islamic and other Middle Eastern faiths don't generally recognize Western festivals, and neither do the governments of the Middle East.

That doesn't mean Halloween doesn't exist there, though. In fact, celebrations are not confined to a handful of Americans in a small communal gathering. In a document posted by the controversial WikiLeaks, a us diplomat provided details of a Halloween party that took place in 2009 at the top levels of Saudi Arabian society. The party was thrown by a member of the royal family and broke numerous Islamic taboos, including that against alcohol (*sadiqi*, a locally produced bootleg liquor, was provided). The event was attended by about 150 young Saudis, nearly all of whom were in costume.[26]

Halloween is basically non-existent in Israel. They do have the celebration of Purim, which is similarly joyful and does offer children the opportunity to dress up in costume. However, Purim – which celebrates a historic deliverance of the Jewish people – is not otherwise similar to Halloween, despite an infamous quote in 2008 from then-presidential candidate Senator John McCain. 'As they celebrate their version of Halloween here, they are somewhere close to a 15-second warning', the Senator noted, referring to the amount of time it takes to escape an attack. Senator Joe Lieberman took the blame for McCain's gaffe, saying that he had attempted to explain Purim to the candidate.[27]

Halloween in East Asia

In East Asia, Halloween has chiefly been welcomed by the two centres of pop culture in Asia: Hong Kong and Japan.

Halloween has been celebrated in former British colony Hong Kong with small parties for at least twenty years, but it received a huge boost in 2007 when Disneyland Hong Kong introduced 'Haunted Halloween'. Strangely enough, the Hong Kong park is the only venue in Disney's chain of amusement parks that has presented actual Halloween mazes and themed areas, complete with live actors and special effects (in addition to the parades and ride makeovers that the other Disney theme parks receive). Disneyland Hong Kong began with two traditional mazes: 'Haunted Hotel' in the park's Main Street area and 'Demon Jungle' in Adventureland. In later years, they added more haunted attractions, including 'Alien Invasion'.

Since Disneyland Hong Kong first began to heavily promote their 'Haunted Halloween', the festival has become very popular throughout Hong Kong. 'Halloween satisfies Hong Kongers need for a) escapism and b) feeling cozy within large crowds', suggested CNN Hong Kong editor Zoe Li in 2010.[28] Hong Kong celebrates with large-scale parties and costume events; the Lan Kwai Fong district is sealed off to traffic for the evening. Many of Hong Kong's restaurants offer special Halloween-themed menus for the evening – even pumpkin-flavoured dishes can be found. The morning after also takes on special significance in Hong Kong, but it has nothing to do with visiting graveyards (an activity saved for the Chinese festivals *Ch'ing Ming*, held in the spring, and *Yue Laan*, in late summer); instead, the socially savvy Hong Kongers will be busy uploading and tagging their costume photos to their favourite online networks.

In mainland China, where both *Ch'ing Ming* and *Yue Laan* are still widely observed, Halloween has just started to become fashionable for a stranger reason than its carnival atmosphere or amusement parks: it's less frightening than *Yue Laan* ('the Hungry Ghost Festival'), when ghosts are believed to walk the streets and are offered food and paper money for use in the afterworld. 'It's really not as much fun as Halloween', noted Beijing website editor Sheila Shi, when explaining why many Chinese young people are showing a preference for Halloween these days.[29] Although large-scale Halloween parties in China are still confined to the major cities, young people around the country are celebrating Halloween online, and websites specializing in e-greeting cards have seen a tremendous upswing in Halloween business since 2006. Halloween decorating is also more popular in many areas of China than costuming or parties (and certainly than trick or treat).

Ever since the company Omotesando organized the first Halloween parade in Japan in 1983, celebration of the day has grown annually. Japan's interest in 'cosplay' (costumed play, usually involving dressing up in imitation of a favourite movie or manga hero or heroine) and festivals has led to the easy acceptance of Halloween. Japanese Studies researcher William Patrick Galbraith explains:

> The *matsuri*, or festival, might be seen as a communal experience that allows behaviours outside rigid behaviours and etiquette, one reason this social pressure release valve has been so crucial in Japan historically.[30]

Halloween costume parades for both adults and children are now popular throughout Japan. Omotesando's 'Hello Halloween Pumpkin Parade' now draws 1,000 costumed Tokyo children, and in Yokohama stores have banded together to offer trick or treat to young visitors. Kawasaki offers a market selling Halloween goods, and Japan has gladly offered up such cultural icons as Hello Kitty to the Halloween merchandising altar. Interest in the history of Halloween is also abundant, and in 2011 several major Japanese newspapers ran articles on Western traditions and lore.

Japanese girls celebrate Halloween, Tokyo, 31 October 2009.

Halloween in the Southern Hemisphere

If Halloween is either already long established or catching on throughout the northern hemisphere, it's not faring so well south of the equator. While this is perhaps unsurprising in areas where Christianity is not the primary religion, it's noteworthy that Australia and New Zealand are the only two major English-speaking regions where Halloween has never taken root. New Zealand has actively celebrated Guy Fawkes/Bonfire Night into modern times, complete with rhyming, begging and 'bangers' (or fireworks), but has virtually no history of Halloween celebrations.

Halloween has chugged along in Australia at a low level, never really being accepted and never quite completely dying out. A few suburban neighbourhoods reported trick or treating activity in the mid-2000s, but the practice seemed to have vanished again by the end of the decade. In October 2010, a seventeen-person group calling itself 'the Halloween Institute' tried to lobby for Australian government recognition of Halloween as a public holiday, but their protests were met with little more than shrugs from Australian retailers and amusement from local media, especially given that the Institute's chairman happened to be the owner of an online Halloween business.

In Africa – where the practice of Christianity continues to rise – All Saints' Day is a public holiday in a few countries, but Halloween only seems to be observed in South Africa. A South African Wiccan has noted that Samhain in the southern hemisphere must be observed at the end of the April, if the 'cycles of nature' are to be properly celebrated.[31] In South Africa, there has been a rise in Halloween celebration, complete with trick or treaters and stores stocking Halloween goods, but there's also been opposition from some Christians. In 2005, the head of the Christian Action Network allegedly decided to protest the 'diabolical' celebration by taking his own children on a paintball shooting spree, with trick or treaters as the targets.

Despite such opposition, Halloween has been increasingly embraced by South African's youth culture. In 2011, there were

Halloween rave parties featuring internationally known recording artists (and makeup artists, who provided guests with a Halloween look free of charge), a ten-day 'Horrorfest' featuring horror movies and Halloween activities, and a 'Halloween Jam' for BMX dirt bike fans, in which many of the riders participated in costume.

Even the parts of South America that are south of the equator have relatively minor observances of Halloween or All Saints' Day; but Central America is home to *Dias de los Muertos*, which is surely among the most extraordinary celebrations on earth.

5

Dias de los Muertos

There is perhaps no better proof that Halloween is a combination of the Celtic Samhain and the Christian All Saints'/All Souls' Day than Central and South America's *Dias de los Muertos* ('Days of the Dead'). Here the Christian observance is stripped of the Celtic influence but combined with other local festivals, and the result is an event which bears only the faintest resemblance to Halloween. There is little emphasis on masking, house-to-house begging, bonfires, pranking, fortune-telling or parties; death is accepted and mocked, not feared. Nor is *Dias de los Muertos* strictly a Catholic holy-day – the proliferation of skull imagery, the seasonal foods and many of the local customs associated with it can only be attributed to the surviving influence of Aztec, Mayan and other Mesoamerican peoples and histories.

At its most basic, *Dias de los Muertos* is a period covering All Saints' and All Souls' Days that pays tribute to deceased loved ones. Sometimes it is a single day – *El Dia de los Muertos* – and takes place on 2 November, but typically it begins at sundown on 31 October and continues through to 2 November. It is celebrated in one form or another throughout most of Central America as well as in a few parts of South America, and it has also made inroads into North America, especially in those areas around the us–Mexico border and in cities with large Latino populations. Probably its most widely known icon is the candy skull, usually about the size of a golf ball and decorated with frosting (icing), glitter or sequins (although it may also have a child's name written on it).

The celebration also typically includes graveyard visits, while in the home an *ofrenda*, or special altar to the dead, may be constructed. The living feast on special foods, and favourite foods are placed out for returning spirits.

Considerable debate has raged recently over how much influence the Celts and Samhain really had on Halloween, and similar arguments occur over Aztec / Mayan / Purepecha vs Christian in regards to *Dias de los Muertos*. As with the Celts, much of our knowledge of Mesoamerican history comes down to us via early Christian missionaries; however, these recordings are comparatively recent – dating back to the sixteenth century – and we also have a great deal of archaeological evidence. We know, for example, that the Aztecs had a complicated religion and a calendar of eighteen months of twenty days each, plus an extra period of five days at the end of the year (there is some speculation that the five-day period, which was essentially a time of rest, was translated to the modern *Dias de los Muertos*[1]). Included in their festivals were two in honour of the dead: *Miccailhuitontli* ('Little Feast of the Dead') and *Miccailhuitl* ('Great Feast of the Dead'), held in the ninth and tenth months of the Aztec calendar, corresponding to August. Also celebrated in the tenth month was *Zocotlhuetzi* ('Great Fall of the Xocotl Fruit'), a harvest festival. These festivals were celebrated with the manufacture of special foods (*tamales*) and decorations (flower garlands made of *zempaschuitl*, or yellow marigold); the ceremonies continued for twenty days, and formed one great celebration of the dead. Games in which young men climbed to the top of a stripped tree to reach an icon made of dough were played, and ancestors were honoured with prayers and feasting.

Another part of the celebration of the Great Feast of the Dead was human sacrifice. History may have clouded over whether the Celts included sacrificial rites during Samhain, but there's no question that it was an important part of *Miccailhuitl*. At the climax of the festival, captives in special paper costumes were led to the *tzompantli*, or skull rack, which held the heads of those previously offered in sacrifices, and then were sacrificed by first being burned, then having their hearts cut out with a ceremonial knife. Finally the bodies were cast down the sides of the pyramidal temple, where the heads were removed and placed in the *tzompantli*.

Death, skull and skeleton iconography figured prominently in the art of both the Aztecs and the Mayans; figurines, pottery and sculpted reliefs all feature skull-faced gods and humans, and may or may not be associated with sacrifice. It seems likely that this proliferation of death and skull imagery became incorporated into modern *Dias de los Muertos* celebrations as the candy skulls and folk art of skeletons. The Catholics weren't alone in using a system of syncretism: the Aztecs often incorporated the religious beliefs of conquered peoples into their system, and their great temple in Tenochtitlan even had a chamber (the *coateocolli*) in which they kept the paraphernalia of other religious systems.[2]

As soon as ten years after Hernán Cortés led the Spanish conquistadors to victory over the Aztec Empire (marching under a banner that read 'We shall conquer under the sign of the cross'), missionaries were arriving in the New World and recording what they saw. Two in particular – Diego Durán and Bernardino de Sahagún – became fluent in the native Nahuatl language, and transcribed much of the existing history and lore. Durán watched newly Christianized natives make offerings to dead children on All Saints' Day and to dead adults on All Souls' Day, and recognized that *Miccailhuitontli* and *Miccailhuitl* had 'been passed to the Feast of Allhallows in order to cover up the ancient ceremony'.[3] Foods and drinks that had been prepared for the old Aztec feasts – chocolate, *tamales*, *pulque* (an alcoholic beverage) – were bequeathed to the new holidays. Some priests tried to make use of old rituals by incorporating them into the new Christian services: one, Pedro de Gante, noted in 1558 that 'in all their adorations of their gods they sang and danced before the gods', and attempted to create new songs for them that honoured God instead.[4] The natives often hid their former beliefs under the guise of Catholicism, and some simply refused to give up their old religion, compromising only when it came to human sacrifice. Another observer, the farmer and author Carl Christian Sartorius, noted in 1858 that with the Mexicans the festival of *todos santos* received a national colouring, dating from the aborigines, but gradually adopted by the Mestizoes ... It is not the festival of the Roman Church, for this is here only a secondary consideration, it is an ancient Indian festival, which the prudence of the Christian priests, who found it too deeply rooted amongst the neophytes, added to the Christian holidays.[5]

Sartorius joins other Europeans in being bewildered by the mood of the celebrants as well:

Neither the Indian nor the Mestizo knows the bitterness of sorrow; he does not fear death; the departure from life is not dreadful in his eyes, he does not crave for the goods he is leaving, and has no care for those who survive him, who have still the fertile earth, and the mild sky.[6]

Ofrendas, or offerings, are one of the most important aspects of *Dias de los Muertos*. These altars vary slightly from region to region but almost always include a table or some sort of platform over which is spread a clean white cloth. On this offerings of food, drink and tobacco are placed for deceased loved ones; it is believed that even though the dead cannot physically partake of these items, they can still enjoy the essence of them. Photos of the deceased or of saints may be included and flowers (typically the yellow-orange *zempaschuitl*) are also arranged on the *ofrenda*, while their petals create a trail leading to the altar. Copal incense is often burned near the *ofrenda*, since the distinctive musky scent and the smoke are thought to help wandering souls find the offerings. Salt is almost always included, since it is considered purifying, and glasses of water are there to quench the spirits' thirst after their long journey from the underworld. The food and drink are consumed by the family on 2 November, since they believe they have shared the food with their deceased loved ones in this way. The practice of the *ofrenda* may actually be Christian in origin, even though it includes figures created from dough (a common Aztec practice) and of course regional

An *ofrenda*.

foods. It may have originated from the use of the catafalque, a bier typically covered in black cloth which was used in All Souls' Day masses, and was sometimes described as being surrounded by candles and food offerings. The use of *ofrendas* was also recorded in colonial-era Spain: in the Castilian province of Zamora, *ofrendas* were created for souls in Purgatory and employed during Easter and All Souls' Day.

The town of Huequechula in the state of Puebla is host to a unique and spectacular form of *ofrenda*: these multi-layered constructions can reach ten feet in height, and are covered in white or pale satin. Decorations consist largely of photos of the deceased and small figures of angels, although the traditional *zempaschuitl* petals surround the base of the *ofrenda* and make a trail out to the street. Visitors to Huequechula are welcomed into the homes of those with displays and urged to make a small donation and to share food (typically bread and hot chocolate) with the family before leaving.

The *zempaschuitl* flower that is so important at *Dias de los Muertos* derives its name from the Nahuatl words for 'twenty' (*zemposalli*) and 'flowers' (*xochitl*), and was believed by the Aztecs to be a gift from Tonatiuh, the sun god, given to them so they would always have something beautiful and gold like the sun to mark the resting places of their late loved ones.[7]

In colonial Mexico, reports on *Dias de los Muertos* celebrations often painted them as raucous, with poorer Mestizos drinking in graveyards; in fact, in 1766, the Royal Office of Crime prohibited cemetery visits during the holiday and tried to control the sale of alcohol. The production of small sugar (or *alfeñique*) animal figures is recorded as early as 1763, but since similar figures are still sold in parts of Italy, and were known to be sold in Spain, this seems to have been a European custom imported to the New World. *Alfeñique* skulls, on the other hand, are not clearly reported until the nineteenth century. In 1841, Madame Calderón de la Barca recorded the first mention of candy skulls when she wrote of walking past the booths of vendors on All Saints' Day and seeing the skulls 'temptingly arranged in grinning rows, to the great edification of the children'.[8] In an article from 1896, a visitor to a small Mexican village named San Elias mentioned not only seeing candy skulls for sale in the marketplace on 1 November, along with candy animals and 'little dough images of a corpse', but then seeing them placed on an *ofrenda* in a home, only to be eaten on the following day. This visitor also believed that *ofrendas* were constructed 'solely by the lower classes, not by the rich'.[9]

By the twentieth century, visitors were flocking to Mexico solely to witness Days of the Dead rituals, and perhaps nowhere became more famed for its beautiful and intricate celebrations than the villages and towns in and surrounding Lake Pátzcuaro in the state of

Michoacán. Pátzcuaro was once the centre of the ancient Purépecha Empire; the Purépecha (also known as the Tarascans) were contemporaries of the Aztecs but were never conquered by them. *Dias de los Muertos* in Patzcuaro begins on 28 October, as decorations and flowers are purchased from the *tianguis* or crafts fair. On 1 November on the Lake Patzcuaro island of Janitzio, the adults wake at sunrise and go to the small village cemetery, where the graves are decorated with *zempaschuitl, pan de muertos* (bread of the dead), fruits and candles, all neatly arranged on clean white cloths. Then the adults step out of the cemetery, and the 'Vigil of the Little Angels' occurs; for the next few hours, the children will watch over the graves and complete the decorating. During the rest of the day, preparations will be made for the evening ritual with the adults: the men use spears to hunt wild duck to be used in the food offerings (600 canoes can bring in 25,000 ducks in a day[10]). In the early part of the evening, boys will engage in a game called *Teruscan*, in which they 'steal' (with permission) food items left for them on the roofs and yards of houses. Ritual dances will be held in the evening, including one called the *pescado blanco*, which pays tribute to the lake's native whitefish. Around midnight, the church bell begins to ring, calling souls back to earth, and the women and children return to the graveyard where they decorate graves and tombs with candles, fruit and candy; the men wait outside the graveyard fences. The beauty of the candlelit night-time cemetery, adorned with flowers and fruits, has become famous around the world; Patzcuaro draws an estimated 100,000 visitors for each Day of the Dead (around one-third come from outside of Mexico), and queues for the small boats that go to Janitzio are long.[11] The small whitefish that once provided much of Janitzio's economy have been fished out for some time, but fishermen still perform with their traditional butterfly nets to earn tips from tourists, so *Dias de los Muertos* has become an important revenue source for Janitzio.

In some areas of Mexico, Days of the Dead begin on 28 October, as those who died in accidents are remembered. Trails of *zempaschuitl* petals can often be found that lead from spots on a road where a loved one has died in a car accident to the home altar. On 29

Day of the Dead altar, Janitzio, Michaoacan, Mexico.

October, those who died a violent death are welcomed, and 30 October sees the return of babies who died before baptism (a small offering for these souls is usually created in a corner of the room, since these unbaptized spirits should not be allowed to approach the main altar). The last day of October marks the arrival of the spirits of children who were baptized, and 1 November is reserved for adults.

In the southeastern Mexican state of Oaxaca, the indigenous people who once ruled the region were the Zapotecs, and the merging of their culture with the Spanish has given rise to *Xandu Ya*, or All Saints'. The Tehuanos, descended from the Zapotecs, set up 'All New Saints' altars for the celebration; they honour the memory of anyone who has died in the previous year, provided that at least 40 days have passed between their death and 30 October. Preparation of the altar is an activity shared among friends and neighbours, who may provide some of the food and drink (these include *atole de leche*, a traditional drink made from corn starch and milk). The altars are prepared in the form of stepped pyramids, with each level representing a different phase of life, as is held by Zapotec beliefs. One local belief is that souls return in the form of butterflies, and so any appearance of a butterfly during *Xandu Ya* is meaningful. The observance ends with the lighting of fireworks. The Tehuanos also visit graveyards throughout the week, and may hire musicians to play music by the side of their loved ones' resting places.

The Tehuanos also have a local legend that is strangely similar to the Breton story of Wilherm Postik, about a man who did not honour his ancestors but drank instead. When he encountered the souls of the dead carrying away their offerings, only his mother held a stone instead of fruit and bread. The man ran home to build an altar to his mother, but he was too late, and was found dead three days later.

In Mexico City, *Dias de los Muertos* is not just a traditional observance, but is also a commercial enterprise, an artistic endeavour and – on occasion – a government project. In 2000, for example, the local government organized a large event called 'Offerings of the Millennium', which included contests, museum exhibits, historical displays and musical performances. Art galleries and museums, including the Diego Rivera Museum, exhibit folk art and special *ofrendas*, and street vendors sell papier mâché toys of skeletons playing musical instruments, eating, mourning one another and just about any other everyday activity imaginable. There are also chocolate and candy skulls for children, and tall candles, copal and *zempaschuitl* for adults.

Calaveras (the Spanish word for skulls) are a form of satirical short poem focusing on death and the macabre popular around Mexico during *Dias de los Muertos. Calaveras* originated in newspapers in the nineteenth century, and first took the form of fake poetic obituaries of then-living public figures, often government officials. Sometimes they poked macabre fun at an entire profession, as in this one entitled 'Neighbourhood Barber':

> You performed many miracles
> With beards and hair,
> So you don't care that
> You're underground:
> You gave some cuts
> To people passing by,
> And now for your stupidity
> You're wrapped in a shroud,
> With a razor and some scissors
> To trim *calaveras*.[12]

In some areas of Mexico, children go through their neighbourhoods on All Saints' or All Souls' Eve reciting *calaveras* in exchange for small rewards of food. The *calaveras* also gave *Dias de los Muertos* its most famous artist in the person of José Guadalupe Posada, whose delightfully morbid engravings often accompanied the short poems in newspapers. Posada's etching 'La Calavera Catrina' of 1913, which depicts a wealthy woman in a flowered hat rendered as a skull, is possibly the single most famous work of art associated with Days of the Dead; Diego Rivera later used Catrina as the centrepiece of his mural 'Dream of a Sunday Afternoon in Alameda Park', and Posada's work was also influential on the muralist José Clemente Orozco.

Twenty-seven miles southwest of Mexico City is Mixquic, where *Dias de los Muertos* is celebrated with one of Mexico's few other examples of begging children: during the evening of 1 November,

José Guadulupe Posada, *La Calavera Catrina*, 1913, zinc etching.

groups of children go from house to house offering prayers, ringing a bell and begging gifts of food. On 2 November, children also engage in *calavereando* or 'skulling' – going from house to house and asking for 'a little skull' (a treat).[13] Tombs in Mixquic are decorated with mosaics made from the petals of *zempaschuitl* and other flowers. The mosaics, of course, often feature skeleton imagery.

In the central Mexican state of San Luis Potosí, one of the main ethnic groups are the Teneks, who are descended from the Mayans but were cut off during the Aztec conquests. The Teneks celebrate All Saints' as *Xantolo*, a name derived from Nahuatl pronunciation of the Latin word for 'saints', *sanctorum*. Some Tenek people don't visit cemeteries during the time of the festival because they believe the spirits of their loved ones are in the homes, visiting the *ofrendas*; others visit on 2 November, when they bury small bits of food in their loved ones' graves. Arches are an important part of *Xantolo*, and are constructed both outside the home and inside, as part of the *ofrenda*. The arches, which represent the thirteen skies found in Aztec beliefs, are made of leafy local branches bent into a curve and decorated with *zempaschuitl* and another local flower called *olotillo*. Coins are included on the altar so that the dead can pay for passage across the Chicuachuapan River in the underworld; however, candy skulls don't appear in this region. On 2 November, the trail of *zempaschuitl* petals that led visiting souls to the *ofrenda* is swept away and replaced with a new trail so that the spirits can find their way back to the afterlife. Visitors to a home are offered food (which has been prepared from pigs, turkeys and chickens that the homeowners purchased in February), and they are expected to drop a small piece first as an offering to the earth. The Tenek also practice traditional dances at *Xantolo* in masks they have sculpted themselves. Characters may include grotesque representations of devils and skeletons. Since women do not take part, female parts are played by male dancers. The dances take place at both the home and the cemetery, and are circular in form, expressing a belief in the circle of life and death.

In the southeastern state of Yucatán, once home to the Mayans, All Saints' is known as *Hanal Pixan* and includes many pre-Hispanic

Wooden devil mask (accented with porcupine quills) from *Dias de los Muertos*.

elements. Here the souls of children are welcomed on 31 October and dismissed on 7 November; the adults arrive on 1 November and depart on 8 November. The offerings include traditional Mayan foods like the drink *el balche*, and *mucbil* chicken, which is cooked by being buried. Many of the decorations centre on green crosses representing the *ceiba* tree, which the Mayans believed was the highway that ran from heaven to the earthly plane and then to the underworld.

These traditions are dying out in many areas of Mexico, and various institutions are now attempting to preserve them by holding *ofrenda* contests each year. These contests usually have several divisions, including traditional and free-style, and also provide an attractive way for tourists to experience *Dias de los Muertos*.

Just to the south of Mexico, in Guatemala, *Dias de los Muertos* is celebrated with *barriletes gigantes*, huge kites which are flown to guide the dead back for the festivities. The kites, which are constructed from bamboo with intricately painted coverings, can be up to seven metres in length and are also presented at contests and fairs. Guatemala also celebrates the holiday with many traditionally Mayan practices, including rituals conducted entirely in Mayan.

Dias de los Muertos is celebrated much more quietly through the rest of Central and South America. In Nicaragua, families spend the night beside the graves of dead loved ones. In Ecuador, food might be eaten next to a grave in the belief that the dead spirit is sharing the meal. In Brazil, *Dia de Finados* takes place only on 2 November and involves simple cemetery visits.

Dias de los Muertos has also begun to appear in more and more American communities, especially those with large Spanish-speaking populations. In communities near the US–Mexico border, it is celebrated in traditional ways, with visits to the graveyards, prayers and feasts. However, in more urban areas, it has become an increasingly cross-cultural and commercialized activity. In San Francisco, a procession and altar exhibit have been held each 2 November since the 1970s; the event takes place in the Mission District and draws 20,000 participants. Celebrations are still small in New York City, with few community-wide events; according to Brooklyn-based

A contemporary Aztec dancer on *Dia de los Muertos*.

author Salvador Olguin, 'The Mexican community here always celebrates this as a private party.'[14] Cities like Houston and Los Angeles hold a number of events, some of which charge admission, and which typically feature *ofrenda* exhibits, folk art, musical performances, face painting and workshops for children.

Halloween has begun to intrude on *Dias de los Muertos* cele-brations, with mixed success. Trick or treat is now practised in parts of Mexico, although the classic phrase has been replaced by the local version: *'queremos* Halloween' ('we want Halloween'). Skeleton and witch costumes are popular, and sometimes the costuming and begging even extends from 30 October to 2 November. The day is occasionally referred to as *Dia de las Brujas* ('Day of the Witches'), and children may be required to perform a small song to obtain a treat. Trick or treating in Mexico seldom involves homes, but is instead conducted around shops.

As Halloween in Mexico began to catch on, both political con-servatives and Mexico's Roman Catholic Church lashed out. In 2007, a columnist in a conservative magazine, *Yo Influyo*, called on teachers to 'eradicate' Halloween and to 'defend our culture'.[15] That same year, the Archdiocese of Mexico proclaimed:

> Those who celebrate Halloween are worshipping a culture of death that is the product of a mix of pagan customs. The worst thing is that this celebration has been identified with neo-pagans, Satanism and occult worship.[16]

Strangely enough, the statement from the Church made no mention of *Dias de los Muertos*.

In 2005 Venezuelan President Hugo Chavez also called for a ban on Halloween, but for unique reasons: he described the festival as a 'game of terror' and said that the American celebration was about 'putting fear into other nations, putting fear into their own people'.[17] Apparently jack-o'-lanterns bearing anti-government messages had been found around the capital, Caracas, shortly before Chavez's statement, although he did not specifically refer to this Halloween trick.

6

From Burns to Burton:
Halloween and Popular Culture

As Halloween has transformed, spread and integrated through the centuries and around the globe, it has become a significant part of every culture that has accepted it. It has not only been defined by customs, politics and art but has sometimes served in part to redefine them. Home celebrations have reflected an area and time's belief in religion and the occult, costuming and trick or treat have become irreversibly interwoven with the media, and books, films and art about Halloween have become their own cottage industries. There's no question that Halloween has inspired popular culture – but to what extent? Would Washington Irving, Robert Burns, John Carpenter, Tim Burton or even Edgar Allan Poe be as widely known without Halloween? What about Stephen King, or zombies? Has Halloween made the entire genre of horror more accepted and popular? Does the goth subculture owe a debt to it? At the heart of all these speculations is one simple question: what does Halloween *really* represent?

The answer to that is that Halloween is – as folklorist and Halloween expert Jack Santino has noted – 'polysemic': it holds different meanings in different places and times, and even to different persons within a single place. To the modern adult American, it's a chance to indulge fears in an environment that is relatively safe, because it's defined by art and imagination. To a contemporary Russian, it's a night on which to exercise freedom of expression. For a Scandinavian, it might be a last celebration before the long, dark winter sets in.

But 500 years ago – in what we might think of as Halloween's infancy – it was perceived very differently. In a world just emerging from the Dark Ages and still under the threat of plague, All Hallows' was a curious and uncertain mix of pagan and Christian, magic and meditation, raucous festival and sombre reflection.

Since Halloween has – at least until very recently – been ephemeral in how it was celebrated, its history must be sought primarily through the arts. Fortunately it has made an impact on poetry, fiction, theatre, film, radio, television, music, painting, graphic design and folk crafts, and has left a well-tracked but winding path along which its evolution may be traced.

The Literature of Halloween

The first modern novel, *Don Quixote*, didn't appear until the same year in which Guy Fawkes attempted to blow up the Houses of Parliament. Before that, the primary literary forms were poetry and drama, and certainly there are plenty of Halloween mentions to be found in both. The Scots were particularly fond of including references to the festival in their poems and ballads. Alexander Montgomerie's 'Montgomeries Answere to Polwart', which contains the first famous reference to Halloween, is actually a playful attack on a rival poet. In effect, Halloween begins its own cultural history as a device for mockery.

The Scottish ballads, however, emphasize the day's romantic side. Although Sir Walter Scott's *Minstrelsy of the Scottish Border* didn't appear until 1802, it did include Scott's own adaptation of the classic 'Tamlane', *c.* 1548. These stanzas from the ballad, as Tamlane tells his love Janet how she might rescue him from the fairies, paint a wild and lovely picture of early Halloweens:

> This night is Hallowe'en, Janet,
>> The morn is Hallowday;
> And, gin ye dare your true love win,
>> Ye hae nae time to stay.

The night it is good Hallowe'en,
  When fairy folk will ride;
And they that wad their true-love win,
  At Miles Cross they maun bide.[1]

Tam goes onto describe what transformations the fairy queen will put him through, and what Janet must do to keep hold of him throughout.

Shakespeare doesn't refer to Halloween often, and when he does it's in a derisive or off-handed manner – understandably, since he was an English playwright during the anti-Catholic and anti-All Saints' Day reigns of Queen Elizabeth and James I – but there are none the less several mentions of it in his works. In *Henry IV Part I* (I,ii), Henry tells Falstaff, 'Farewell, thou latter spring; farewell, All-hallown Summer!', referring to the warm period often found towards the end of October. In *Two Gentlemen of Verona* (II,I), the character Speed accuses someone of 'puling like a beggar at Hallowmass'. *Richard II* contains these lines:

She came adorned hither like sweet May;
Sent back like Hallowmas, or short'st of day (V,i).

For nearly two centuries, Halloween would virtually disappear from literature, as the British Isles were ruled by Protestants. Celebrating it was banned in 1647, when Parliament abolished all festivals but Guy Fawkes Day/Night. But in the late eighteenth century, as Scottish nationalism grew, the Scots once again turned a poetic eye to Halloween. Robert Burns, of course, provided the most famous example in 1785 with 'Hallowe'en', a poem which surely did more to influence generations of Halloween revellers than any other single work. The Burns poem, with its detailed descriptions of fortune-telling, food and flirtation, was quoted throughout the nineteenth century in virtually all the popular almanacs and miscellanies. In the edition of his *Book of Days* published in 1832, for instance, Robert Chambers quoted from the Burns poem at length, and even addressed what it omits:

It is somewhat remarkable, that the sport of ducking for apples is not mentioned by Burns, whose celebrated poem of Halloween presents so graphic a picture of the ceremonies practised on that evening in the west of Scotland, in the poet's day.[2]

In 1898, Martha Russell Orne also quoted Burns in describing party games in her *Hallowe'en: How to Celebrate It*; most of the party pamphlets that would follow over the next three decades would continue to refer to Burns, even though their intended readers were middle-class, urbanized Americans.

Halloween made few appearances in the burgeoning Gothic literature movement, probably because most of the practitioners were British. However, it does feature prominently in the influential collection *Tales of Wonder* (1801), often considered a landmark work in the history of Gothic literature and poetry. The anthology was compiled by Matthew G. Lewis, the author of what many consider to be the most outstanding work of the entire Gothic movement, the novel *The Monk* (1796). After residing at Bothwell Castle in Scotland, the English Lewis was inspired to write 'Bothwell Bonny Jane', a poem which employs the form of the traditional Scottish ballad as well as the Scottish inclination towards the supernatural. Lewis chose the poem to open *Tales of Wonder* and it has since been frequently quoted, especially for its references to Halloween. The mock ballad tells of Bonny Jane, whose father intends to marry her to the wealthy Lord Malcolm, but Jane would prefer a life of poverty with Edgar, a local peasant. A sympathetic friar hears her plea and agrees to help her. On Halloween night, he escorts her to the River Clyde, and reveals that he himself is in love with her. He kidnaps her and puts her in a boat to cross the river, but a terrible storm arises; the boatman tells the monk that they must lighten the boat's weight, and the monk hurls Jane into the water. The boatman then reveals himself as a demon; he clasps the monk to him and they sink into the stormy water. Many years later, the legend of the monk and bonny Jane lives on:

> Yet legends say, at Hallow-E'en,
>> When Silence holds her deepest reign,
> That still the ferryman-fiend is seen
>> To waft the monk and bonny Jane . . . [3]

Even though *Tales of Wonder* was first published sixteen years after the Burns poem, Lewis felt the need to explain Halloween to his readers. The poem's first mention of Halloween has been footnoted by Lewis: 'On this night witches, devils, &c. are thought, by the Scotch, to be abroad on their baneful errands. See Burns's Poem, under the title of "Hallow-E'en".'[4]

Two years after Lewis released his *Tales*, Sir Walter Scott had published all three volumes of his collection *Minstrelsy of the Scottish Border*, which included not just 'Tamlane' but several other works that referenced Halloween. In his lengthy introduction to 'Tamlane', for example, Scott discusses the sixteenth-century case of accused witch Alison Pearson, and a satirical poem of the period that was written about her supposed relationship with a prominent bishop. In the poem, the Bishop is described as going to attend a meeting with witches 'On horsback on Hallow ewin',[5] providing further proof of how the festival had already been linked to witches and diabolical doings by the end of the 1600s.

In 1820, Scott published his novel *The Monastery*, which despite being principally a historical novel includes many elements of the Gothic (one of the main characters is a ghost called the White Lady). It contains a direct Halloween element, since the protagonist, Mary Avenel, was born on Halloween. As Scott describes her in one encounter, 'Something also had transpired concerning her being born on All-hallow Eve, and the powers with which that circumstance was supposed to invest her over the invisible world.'[6] *The Monastery* could arguably be called the first Halloween novel.

Two other poems of the mid-nineteenth century are especially worth mentioning: the first, *Halloween: A Romaunt*, by an Episcopal bishop named Arthur Cleveland Coxe, is really a Christian devotional that contains a few brief references to Halloween. However, these references suggest that by 1842, when the poem was first privately published in America, Coxe's readers would have been familiar enough with Halloween to understand:

> 'Tis the night – the night
> Of the grave's delight,
>   And the warlocks are at their play!
> Ye think that without,
> The wild winds shout,
> But no, it is they – it is they![7]

More interesting, if less direct in its references to Halloween, is Edgar Allan Poe's 'Ulalume'. The poem recalls a 'night in the lonesome October' as the narrator wanders 'the ghoul-haunted woodland of Weir', thinking of a lost love. These lines strongly suggest that the night is Halloween:

> For we knew not the month was October,
> And we marked not the night of the year –
> (Ah, night of all nights in the year!)[8]

When the narrator stumbles on the vault of his Ulalume, he remembers that it was 'On *this* very night of last year' that he brought his beloved to her vault.[9] 'Ulalume' may or may not actually be set on Halloween, but it has often been recited on the night in question.

However, it's another work by Poe that, despite no reference whatsoever to Halloween, has become so intertwined with it that it's difficult to say whether the story has contributed more to the festival, or vice versa: 'The Black Cat', Poe's classic story from 1843 of madness and murder. The well-known tale of an alcoholic who walls up a cat with the body of his murdered wife does include a reference to witches ('my wife, who at heart was not a little tinctured with superstition, made frequent allusion to the ancient popular notion, which regarded all black cats as witches in disguise'[10]), and has become a classic Halloween reading, especially among schoolteachers looking for Halloween entertainment. Certainly Poe's

Harry Clarke's illustration of Edgar Allan Poe's *The Black Cat*.

entire catalogue is well-suited to the holiday, and as America's first
and greatest author of horror tales it was perhaps inevitable that
Poe and Halloween should mix. However, it is the only Poe story
that appears as a recommended Halloween reading in such seminal
early Halloween books as Ruth E. Kelley's *The Book of Hallowe'en*

(1919) and Robert Haven Schauffler's *Hallowe'en* (1935), which reprints the story in its entirety. 'The Black Cat' has almost certainly contributed to the popularity of a major icon for Halloween, which in turn has increased the story's popularity.

If one could choose only three stories that have both contributed greatly to Halloween and have in turn continued to be read and enjoyed year after year thanks to the celebration, the second would be Nathaniel Hawthorne's 'Young Goodman Brown' (1835). As with 'Ulalume', there is no direct naming of Halloween, but the night is strongly implied when the story begins with young newly-wed Faith pleading with her husband, 'Pray tarry with me this night, dear husband, of all nights in the year.'[11] The story describes how the eponymous hero, on a mysterious night-time journey through dark woods, encounters the Devil and learns that the most pious members of his community – Salem – are in fact in league with the Devil, and are all on their way to a diabolical meeting. The story includes frightening imagery of supernatural occurrences (Satan walks with a staff made of a living snake, an overhead cloud is full of voices, a flaming rock holds a baptismal font of blood) and a dismal ending that is a testament to Hawthorne's guilt over the in-volvement of his own great-great-grandfather in the Salem witch trials. 'Young Goodman Browne' has long been a popular Hallow-een story, and has probably helped to promote the icon of the witch, just as 'The Black Cat' served to elevate its title animal to Hal-loween superstar.

The final story in the Halloween triple crown of fiction is Washington Irving's 'The Legend of Sleepy Hollow'. First pub-lished in 1820, the tale of gangly school teacher Ichabod Crane's encounter with the Headless Horseman makes no reference to Hal-loween, although it makes considerable use of an autumn setting, describing the seasonal countryside, harvest and a party. It has become a Halloween classic because of its use of a pumpkin – the Horse-man (who is likely Ichabod's rival Brom Bones in disguise) cradles his 'head' as he rides, and finally hurls it at the terrified teacher, but the next day all that's found are 'the hat of the unfortunate Ichabod, and close beside it a shattered pumpkin'.[12] Did Irving's classic, in which a pumpkin serves as the head of a dreadful goblin, help to seat the jack-o'-lantern on the throne as the undisputed king of Halloween icons? Certainly, 'The Black Cat', 'Young Goodman Brown' and 'The Legend of Sleepy Hollow' have appeared in more American school textbooks as Halloween selections than any other works of prose, and it's surely no coincidence that their three respective subjects – black cats, witches and pumpkins – have become the three main symbols of Halloween.

Another of Irving's tales is also set on 'a fine autumnal day' and is a Halloween favourite: 'Rip Van Winkle'.[13] This classic tells the story of a man who, while wondering in the mountains one day, encounters a strange group of little bearded men. Rip sips from their keg, falls asleep and awakens twenty years later. Similarities to classic fairy tales set at Samhain or Halloween are obvious: a lone mortal has stumbled on a supernatural gathering and upon returning to his own world finds that time has moved on without him.

By the mid-nineteenth century, a new form of popular entertainment had taken hold thanks to advances in printing and distribution techniques: the magazine. By 1850, more than 600 magazines were being printed in the u.s., all hungry for content. In 1830, the first magazine that targeted women began: *Godey's Ladies Book*, which early on acquired Sarah J. Hale as editor. Ironically, Hale would go on to be remembered for her involvement with another festival – she campaigned to have Thanksgiving recognized as a national American holiday – but *Godey's* was one of many nineteenth-century periodicals that featured Halloween-themed pieces in its pages. 'Halloween, or Chrissie's Fate' by Meta G. Adams is a typical example of the quaint Halloween stories to be found in American magazines of the 1870s and '80s. First published in 1871 in *Scribner's Monthly Magazine* (and reprinted a year later in *The Century*), Halloween is apparently unknown to the story's elderly spinster narrator until the arrival of a youngster:

> So it came to pass that my niece Kitty Coles was spending
> the month with me, and having happened upon an old book

upon 'The Supernatural', had become imbued with a frantic desire to test some of her newfound theories on the approaching 'Halloween.'[14]

The party consists entirely of girls (age is never specified, although they are described as 'young' and 'girlish'), and activities include pouring melted lead into water to read the shapes, naming chestnuts in pairs and burning them on the hearth, and (after a frightful walk through a deserted wing of the spinster's house) eating an apple before a mirror at midnight. One of the girls, Chrissie, encounters a wraith while at the mirror, and the rest of the story is a standard nineteenth-century romance, as Chrissie finally meets and weds the man she encountered via a mirror's reflection on Halloween night.'

Not all the Halloween-themed pieces found in these magazines were short stories; many took the form of non-fiction accounts of folklore beliefs. In 1886, for example, *Harper's New Monthly Magazine* ran 'Halloween: A Threefold Chronicle' by William Sharp. The sections in this triptych are titled 'Halloween in Ireland', 'Halloween in Scotland' and 'At Sea', which describes a Halloween spent in stormy weather near the Cape of Good Hope:

> The only custom it was in our power to observe was that of dipping for apples; this, however, would prove impossible unless the sea greatly moderated, for it was all the steadiest of us could do to keep our feet at all.[15]

Later the weather calms enough to allow for bobbing, followed by music, dancing and telling of eerie tales.

These magazines probably provided many Americans with their introduction to Halloween, and no doubt housewives were charmed by the descriptions of the parties. America was becoming more industrialized and urbanized, and the middle class, who now had disposable income, were happy to follow in the footsteps of their British kin, whom they still saw as sophisticated older cousins. It's probably no coincidence that Meta G. Adams's 'Halloween, or

Chrissie's Fate' was published two years after Queen Victoria's Halloween visit to Balmoral Castle, an event that was widely reported in the American press.

It was also about this time that a small explosion of works exploring folklore of the British Isles appeared. Over the space of seventeen years, dozens of small, regional histories were recorded, and many of the key major studies: Lady Wilde (mother to Oscar) published *Ancient Legends, Mystic Charms, and Superstitions of Ireland* in 1887 and *Ancient Cures, Charms, and Usages in Ireland* in 1890, and introduced readers to stories of fetches and Halloween mischief. Sir James G. Frazer focused on Halloween bonfires and saw Halloween as a Celtic celebration of winter's approach when he published the first edition of *The Golden Bough* in 1890; Douglas Hyde's *Beside the Fire: A Collection of Irish Gaelic Folk Stories* came out in 1890, and included the whimsical folk tale 'Guleesh na Guss Dhu', about a peasant boy who rides with fairies on Halloween night. Sidney Oldall Addy's *Household Tales with Other Traditional Remains* (1895), John Gregorson Campbell's *Superstitions of the Highlands and Islands of Scotland* (1900), T. F. Thistelton Dyer's *British Popular Customs: Present and Past* (1900) and Sir John Rhys's *Celtic Folklore, Welsh and Manx* (1901) all included a wealth of Halloween folk beliefs and stories of malicious spirits. Lady Gregory published *Cuchulain of Muirthemne: The Story of the Men of the Red Branch of Ulster* in 1902 and *Gods and Fighting Men: The Story of the Tuatha de Danaan and of the Fianna of Ireland* in 1904, offering one of the most extensive collections to date of Celtic legends and Samhain lore. By the end of the trend, readers had been introduced to Scottish superstitions, pookas, fire customs, talking corpses on Samhain eve and fairies in every conceivable shape and mood.

It wasn't just that Halloween had arrived; more specifically, American interest in Halloween had arrived. By the end of the nineteenth century, Americans were ready for a book focused solely on Halloween. And in 1898, the Fitzgerald Publishing Company in New York gave them exactly what they wanted with the publication of the first book devoted solely to the celebration of Halloween:

Martha Russell Orne's *Hallowe'en: How to Celebrate It*. This slender, 48-page pamphlet opens with a brief discussion of Halloween history, but spends the bulk of its time focusing on home decoration, preparing invitations and party games, as already mentioned. Although it borrows liberally from Burns and John Gay's *The Shepherd's Week*, there's no question that it is intended for American women: the sample invitations all include American-style addresses ('441 Columbus Ave.'), there are jokes made about famous American historical figures (one party suggestion is that guests each be given a white sheet upon entering and introduced to one another with such epithets as, 'This is my great-uncle who died in 1798; he was an intimate friend of George Washington'[16]); and of course pumpkins – not turnips – figure prominently throughout.

Hallowe'en: How to Celebrate It inaugurated a torrent of similar party pamphlets over the next three decades, and it didn't take long for them to eclipse Orne's work: by 1903, *Werner's Readings and Recitations: Hallowe'en Festivities* spanned 192 pages of 'Entertainments', 'Recitations', 'Ghost Stories', 'Hallowe'en Recipes', and 'Games'. The book's opening line gives some idea of how Halloween was viewed at this time:

> Hallowe'en, or All Hallow Even, the name given to the night of October 31, and the eve of All Saints' Day (November 1), is one of the most delightful opportunities for entertaining. On such a night there should be nothing but laughter, jollity, and mystery.[17]

The section on decorations mentions jack-o'-lanterns frequently, but includes this note: 'Jack-o'-lanterns are made by removing pulp from apples, cucumbers, squashes, pumpkins, etc., cutting places for eyes, nose, and mouth, and fastening a lighted candle inside.'[18] The suggested programme for a typical Halloween party also provides a look at some of the very different ways in which parties were celebrated at the turn of the century, complete with actual theatrical performances to be staged in either the barn or parlour:

Reception and Introduction of Guests
Shadow Pantomimes
Spook March
Witches' Dance
Goblin Parade
Play: 'Clever Matchmakers'
Games and Mysteries for Early Evening
March to Supper
Supper and Supper Games
After-Supper Sports, Test, Mysteries
Your Lucky Sticks
Fagot Ghost Stories
Fortune Telling
Games
Home Tests[19]

This book is plainly intended for adults; the short play 'Clever Matchmakers', for instance, is about a middle-aged couple anxious to marry off their daughter, who has almost reached the age of 30.

By the mid-1920s, there were more booklets about Halloween entertaining being published than ever, but now 50 per cent of their space was given over to activities for children. These activities were usually fairly large in scale, suggesting that they were probably meant to be performed in schools or civic settings rather than homes. The activities included recitations, skits or short plays and drills, like 'The Jack-o'-Lantern Drill' from a 1926 booklet:

This is a simple little drill arranged especially for small boys. The boys wear ordinary suits or Hallowe'en costumes, according to tastes and opportunities. The lanterns are not lighted, but red paper is placed over the openings on the inside to simulate light. Lively music. The boys enter from opposite sides of the stage, half on the right, half on the left. They swing their lanterns as they come, in time to the music, and meet at center of the front line.[20]

Cover to the Halloween pamphlet *The Best Halloween Book* (1931), by Lenore K. Dolan.

This drill goes on to delineate 31 separate movements the boys were to make in unison before departing the stage; one can only imagine how anxious those lads must have been to go pranking later that night and put the drill behind them.

By the 1930s, Halloween books were largely or entirely for children, and fortune-telling was dismissed as a superstition from the past. A poem of 1936 entitled 'Her Opinion' opens with this stanza:

> When Mother was a little girl,
> Halloween tricks she used to try,

Chestnuts roast and parings twirl –
As silly, then, as you or I.[21]

Pranking figures more prominently in these booklets as time goes on, with plays and recitations in the later books often mentioning the practice. Sometimes it's dismissed as an innocent boys' activity, with the line 'Boys will be boys' often providing a conclusion, but other poems and skits offer up warnings against the practice, as in the short poem 'The Tale of the Jack-o'-Lantern' from 1937:

A Jack-o'-Lantern played some pranks
One moonlit Hallowe'en,
He started out all by himself
Determined to be mean.

After scaring kittens, puppies and even human babies, the narrator makes the mistake of trying to frighten a witch's black cat:

Its mistress witch then came to sight
And whacked him with her broom,
So that is how one pumpkin head
Was cracked unto his doom.[22]

The end of consumer interest in pamphlets largely came as Halloween moved into being almost completely a children's celebration, and one oriented towards controlling destructive pranking. Tellingly, Dennison's stopped producing its *Bogie Books* in 1934, suggesting that the era of adult Halloween parties and decorations had faded. One of the last of the pamphlets, the *Halloween Fun Book*, was produced in 1937: its introduction advises: 'Instead of condemnation for pranks which too often overstepped the line, youth should be given the cooperation of their parents and leaders in making Hallowe'en a gala, carefree holiday.'[23] The same booklet includes detailed descriptions of house-to-house parties and costuming events, all of which led shortly afterwards to trick or treating.

These pamphlets also suggest a timeline for the evolution of the word 'Halloween': up until 1937, the word nearly always includes the apostrophe that omits the 'v' – 'Hallowe'en' – but the apostrophe begins to vanish from then on. It would still occasionally appear in use through the rest of the 1930s and into the '40s, but seems to have been completely dropped by about 1948.

In 1919, while housewives were apparently buying up Halloween entertainment pamphlets and getting small doses of Halloween history (if they bothered to read the introductions), a 26-year-old American librarian named Ruth Edna Kelley literally made Halloween history by writing *The Book of Hallowe'en*, the first serious historical treatment of the festival. The publisher was no paper goods company or novelties publisher, but Lothrop, Lee & Shepard, a long-established company that had emphasized children's books, literature and mythology. They obviously took *The Book of Hallowe'en* very seriously, releasing it with a lovely gilt-decorated binding, illustrations, an index and even bibliographic references. Kelley makes it clear in her preface that this is not just another party book: 'Those who wish suggestions for readings, recitations, plays, and parties, will find the lists in the appendix useful, in addition to the books on entertainments and games to be found in any public library.'[24] Her history is good overall (she correctly notes Samhain as 'Summer's End'), and is in fact sometimes more accurate than books that came after. Related subjects – 'Witches' and 'Walpurgis Night' – each receive their own chapters, while the bulk of the book assembles old superstitions and folklore related to Halloween. One of the most interesting passages in the book is the paragraph with which it closes: after a discussion of fortune-telling customs still in use at the time in American Halloween parties, Kelley notes:

A far more interesting development of the Hallowe'en idea than these innocent but colorless superstitions, is promised by the pageant at Fort Worth Texas, on October thirty-first 1916. In the masque and pageant of the afternoon four thousand school children took part. At night scenes from the pageant

First edition
cover, 1919, for
Ruth E. Kelley's
*The Book of
Hallowe'en*.

were staged on floats which passed along the streets. The subject was *Preparedness for Peace*, and comprised scenes from
American history in which peace played an honorable part.
Such were: the conference of William Penn and the Quakers
with the Indians, and the opening of the East to American
trade. This is not a subject limited to performances at Hallow-
tide. May there not be written and presented in America a
truly Hallowe'en pageant, illustrating and befitting its noble
origin, and making its place secure among the holidays of
the year?[25]

Kelley would undoubtedly have approved of the Greenwich Village Halloween parade, and would be happy to know that her book is now widely reprinted in both electronic form (it can be found online at such sites as Gutenberg.org) and in hard copy. Original printings of the book are now among the most sought-after of Halloween collectibles, and can command four-figure price tags if the original paper jacket is included.

For over 30 years, Kelley's book stood alone as the only comprehensive source of Halloween history. Then, in 1950, the Henry Schuman publishing company released *Halloween Through Twenty Centuries* by Ralph and Adelin Linton as part of their 'Great Religious Festivals' books – and nearly set Halloween scholarship back forever. Neither as lengthy (108 pages) nor as obviously thoughtfully presented (there is no bibliography or appendix, and only a two-page index) as *The Book of Hallowe'en*, *Halloween Through Twenty Centuries* is a curious and repulsive mix of fact and misinformation so sensationalized that it could best be described as horror fiction. The third sentence of the book states that Halloween 'commemorates beings and rites with which the church has always been at war', and of course the Celts are savages who sacrificed horses and human beings at Samhain until 'this horrid practice was outlawed by Roman command' (the Romans, of course, never conquered Ireland or the Irish Celts).[26] The book is most shocking, however, in apparently either upholding the witch persecutions of the Middle Ages – when at least 40,000 supposed witches were executed, most by being burned alive at the stake – or dismissing them as mere human nature: 'We cannot be too scornful of the excesses of former times, for at times of fear and chaos we do our own witch hunting.'[27] Witchcraft is described as 'an organized cult in opposition to the church', and it is claimed that 'these followers of Satan served their master with devotion and met their death unrepentant'.[28] The book is even illustrated with numerous drawings and paintings of witches celebrating, practising their black arts and of course being executed.

Unfortunately, the Linton book found its way onto many library shelves, and stood alongside Kelley's for the next 40 years as the two books solely focusing on the historical aspect of Halloween. Ironically, *Halloween Through Twenty Centuries* offers an explanation of the appeal of witchcraft that could be equally well applied to why the book found favour with many readers over the years: 'To many peasant folk, the excitement and ecstasy of the Witches' Sabbaths had more appeal than the droning monotony of the church services.'[29] The Linton book would go on to become the standard reference source for generations of evangelical Christians seeking to prove that Halloween was (as the Lintons themselves sum it up in their book's conclusion) 'a degenerate holiday'.[30] Kelley's sober and more accurate portrayal obviously held less appeal for those predisposed towards fire and brimstone.

For the next 40 years, Halloween history was confined to either magazine articles or playful children's books with colourful illustrations. Then – as the celebration became more popular again with adults – that thankfully changed in 1990, with the publication of Lesley Pratt Bannatyne's *Halloween: An American Holiday, an American History*. For the first time, Halloween had a modern history that was comprehensive, well-researched and entertaining. While it may have been too late to sway some readers away from the Linton book, *Halloween: An American Holiday, an American History* ushered in a new era of scholarly interest in Halloween. It was followed in 1994 by the first collection of academic papers: *Halloween and Other Festivals of Death and Life*, edited by Jack Santino; in 2002 by David J. Skal's *Death Makes a Holiday: A Cultural History of Halloween*, the first Halloween history to be published by a major New York publisher (Bloomsbury); in 2003 by *The Halloween Encyclopedia*, the first encyclopaedic reference work on the day; and in 2005 by *Halloween in der Steiermark und anderswo*, the first collection of academic papers to focus on European celebrations of Halloween.

Even given that the modern study of popular culture is essentially less than 40 years old, it's none the less surprising that Halloween has yet to be much dissected in the world of academia. There are, for example, more critical analyses published and university courses taught on *Buffy the Vampire Slayer* than on Halloween. The first (and so far only) academic conference on Halloween was held at Glasgow Caledonian University in Scotland in 2006, and included participants from universities around the world. 'Halloween remains a surprisingly under-researched and under-theorized topic in academic writing', noted the conference's website.[31] Whether the lack of Halloween critical studies is the result of academic disinterest or the fact that Halloween has been so thoroughly integrated into any number of other topics remains an unanswerable question, but given Halloween's burgeoning global popularity, academia will surely begin to take it more seriously in the very near future.

If popular culture theorists have been slow to recognize Halloween's importance, popular culture collectors certainly haven't. In 1995, another cycle in Halloween publishing began with the release of two books: *Halloween Collectables: A Price Guide* by Dan and Pauline Campanelli, and *Halloween in America: A Collector's Guide with Prices* by Stuart Schneider. Halloween collecting had first been recognized in print form in 1984, when Pamela Apkarian-Russell started publishing a newsletter called *The Trick or Treat Trader*, and indeed, in the introduction to his book Schneider mentions collectors who have been searching for particular items for twenty years, and notes that 'time has proved them to be visionaries'.[32] Just as items like comic books, movie posters and trading cards have become highly valued by aging baby boomers, so have vintage Halloween materials. The Campanellis sum it up in the introduction to their book:

> Many of us seem to recall another Halloween from another place and time. There seems to be a Halloween from the innocence of our childhood, filled with candy corn and jack-o'-lanterns and candy wrapped in orange napkins printed with black cats and flying witches. The memory of it gives us comfort ...[33]

Both books are lengthy and focus on colour photographs of particular pieces with detailed descriptions that mention the year and place of manufacture and the name of the manufacturer. Halloween collectors may specialize in one area – postcards, for example, or any items depicting cats – or may simply acquire any and all vintage Halloween items. Some enthusiasts focus on certain companies – Beistle or Dennison's paper decorations are highly sought after, especially Dennison's *Bogie Books* (the first *Bogie Book*, from 1909, may fetch in excess of $2,000 in good condition). The *Bogie Books* are perhaps unique among Halloween collectables in offering Halloween graphics in a Jazz Age setting, showing sophisticated flappers with bobbed hair cavorting in decorated ballrooms. Figural candles from Gurley, metal noisemakers from Kirchhof or US Metal Toy Co., postcards from Winsch or Raphael Tuck (or from particular artists like Ellen Clapsaddle, known for her depictions of idealized children), and early jack-o'-lanterns or candy containers in composition material or papier mâché (with no manufacturer listed) all capture the day's visual appeal, featuring ghosts, witches and pumpkin-headed goblins in vivid autumn colours. Some collectors focus on costumes from manufacturers like Collegeville or Ben Cooper; a rayon costume with garish graphics complete with plastic mask in its original box evokes childhood memories of trick or treat, and may include the bonus of depicting a favourite television, movie or children's book character. Halloween retailing has not been confined to creating items that might be collectable in the future, since some contemporary companies have also taken advantage of the zeal for Halloween collecting by deliberately creating higher-priced instant collectables: Department 56 makes detailed ceramic recreations of whimsical haunted buildings, Disney has released a tidal wave of *Nightmare Before Christmas* material and Mattel has recreated its venerable Barbie doll as a yearly Halloween figure. Reproductions of vintage material are also now widely available, and occasionally fool even the wariest of collectors.

It's probably no coincidence that 1995 was also the first year of ebay, the auction website that swiftly became the world's biggest garage sale and made buying and selling of vintage items available on a global scale. Now that Halloween collectibles had been codified and evaluated in print, collectors began to gorge themselves and

prices rose sharply. The next decade saw a wealth of books on Hallow-
een collectables published, including such specific titles as *Halloween
Favorites in Plastic* and *Timeless Halloween Collectibles, 1920–1949:
A Halloween Reference Book from the Beistle Company Archives With
Price Guide.* Apkarian-Russell, who probably owns the world's largest
Halloween collection, not only contributed three books on the subject (*Collectible Halloween*, 1997; *More Halloween Collectibles: Anthro-
pomorphic Vegetables and Fruits of Halloween*, 1998; and *Halloween:
Collectible Decorations and Games*, 2000) but went on to open the
world's first Halloween museum: The Castle Halloween Museum
in Benwood, Virginia, which is housed in a former school building
and holds over 35,000 pieces.

Halloween fiction also came into its own in the twentieth
century. The first novel to feature the festival's name, *Hallowe'en* by
Leslie Burgess, was published in 1941, and although it was a slight
mystery with a heavy debt to Daphne du Maurier's *Rebecca* it did

Vintage Halloween paper decoration, *c.* 1940.

at least centre on the day itself and included references to Scottish rituals. Four years later, the fantasy writer Charles Williams, who belonged to the literary group the Inklings with J.R.R. Tolkien and C. S. Lewis, produced the supernatural dark fantasy *All Hallows' Eve*, which could perhaps be thought of as the first novel of horror to focus on Halloween. It wasn't until 1972, though, that Ray Bradbury produced what many consider the ultimate Halloween novel: *The Halloween Tree*, which offers a fictionalized history of Halloween in the story of a group of trick or treating boys who are whisked away on a time-travelling adventure by the mysterious Carapace Clavicle Moundshroud. Bradbury, who had touched on Halloween in his earlier classic novel *Something Wicked This Way Comes*, here turns his poetic sensibilities fully on it: 'Night and day. Summer and winter, boys. Seedtime and harvest. Life and death. That's what Halloween is, all rolled up in one', Moundshroud tells the boys at the end of their adventure.[34] In an interview in 2004, Bradbury recalled that *The Halloween Tree* came about in response to the animated television show *It's the Great Pumpkin, Charlie Brown*: Bradbury felt that show had seriously erred in never actually showing the Great Pumpkin, and when he met up with animator Chuck Jones and found that Jones agreed, they set out to produce an animated special that would depict what they felt was the real 'spirit of Halloween'.[35] Bradbury wrote a screenplay, but after production fell through he finally turned his script into the novel, which was eventually turned into an award-winning animated short in 1993. The book, which also includes illustrations by Joseph Mugnaini, has remained in print since its first publication.

The social revolutions of the 1960s and '70s were not confined to civil rights and women's liberation, but spread to pop culture and gave birth to a new era of relaxed standards and more explicit sex and violence. No genre was as impacted by these cultural shifts as horror. Gone were the polite cobwebbed castles and thunderstorms of yore; in their place, films like George Romero's *Night of the Living Dead* and Richard Donner's big-budget hit *The Omen* offered gruesome scenes of cannibalism, dismemberments and beheadings, while the new bestselling novels tackled former taboos like foul-mouthed children (William Peter Blatty's *The Exorcist*) and religiously repressed sexuality (Stephen King's *Carrie*). Given Halloween's existing ties to horror, it seemed likely that Halloween would also begin to figure more in the immensely popular new horror films and fiction, but this was slow in coming. The trick or treaters of the 1950s were now nostalgic adults, and perhaps their warm memories of Halloween were *too* taboo; some Halloween collectors, like Pamela Apkarian-Russell, have reflected this in stating that they have no interest in modern gore-heavy haunted attractions. In the mid-1970s, Halloween fear was still related to the pleasurable tingle, not the terrified scream.

Of course all that would change in 1979, when John Carpenter's *Halloween* rampaged through cinemas, meshing the new explicit horror with the festival of fear, but references to the day seemed confined to film. There were, of course, brief appearances and the occasional novel, but it wasn't until the 2000s that a new cycle of Halloween fiction suddenly appeared. The kick-off point may have been an anthology called *October Dreams: A Celebration of Halloween*, edited by Richard Chizmar and Robert Morrish. This massive, 660-page volume mixed reprinted and original Halloween short stories with authors recalling favourite Halloween memories and essays about Halloween's role in fiction and film. After the release of *October Dreams*, books like Norman Partridge's award-winning *Dark Harvest* used Halloween to explore the dark underside of the myth of idyllic small-town America, and other authors even began to make Halloween fiction their mainstay (Al Sarrantonio, for example, and his cycle of books and stories set in the fictional Halloween town of Orangefield). Halloween has also proven a gold mine for small press publishers in the horror genre, many of whom now include special annual Halloween releases, frequently offered only in expensive signed and limited editions, in their catalogues.

Halloween has arguably always found a more comfortable fictional home in short stories than novels. Virtually every major horror author of the twentieth and twenty-first centuries has explored Halloween in fiction (usually short fiction), and non-genre authors including James Joyce ('Clay', 1914) and Edith Wharton ('All

Cover to 2000's *October Dreams*.

Souls", 1937) have also appropriated it, although they often seem to continue the nineteenth-century notion that Halloween celebrations are the province of rustic servants. One of the first short stories set during a bourgeois Halloween celebration was Robert Bloch's 'The Cloak' (1939), a witty and eerie tale of a man who attends an upscale Halloween party in a rented vampire costume and finds he has an urge to drink blood. By 1948, the festival was firmly entrenched in the middle class, as in Ray Bradbury's 'The October Game', which plays on the Halloween party tradition of passing around various food items in the dark (peeled grapes, wet spaghetti and so on) and pretending they're body parts. In 1964's 'Heavy Set' by Bradbury, Halloween is an accepted suburban ritual that causes a disturbed body-builder to turn on his mother after being humiliated at a party.

The best Halloween stories of the twenty-first century seem to have turned away from the lighter, sometimes humorous fiction of the Blochs and Bradburys and focused on bleak tales that comment on isolation and alienation: examples would be Jack Ketchum's 'Gone' (2000), about a strange encounter between some trick or treaters and a woman who lost her own child; and 'Mr Dark's Carnival' (also 2000), Glen Hirshberg's novella about a folklore professor who finds a legendary haunted house in an isolated patch of Montana prairie, where nineteenth-century frontier justice has given way to the haunted attraction's strange and bloody horrors. The new Halloween fiction is less concerned with class than disillusionment, cannily using baby-boomer nostalgia to turn childhood memories and expectations inside-out.

No discussion of Halloween books would be complete without mentioning those for children, although a comprehensive list of these would be a book itself. Halloween stories for children have of course been around as long as the holiday itself, and once took the form of folklore and fairy tales. In 1833, a Scottish explorer in Canada, J. E. Alexander, spent 31 October in the wilderness and recalled:

> We spent the evening of Halloween among drowned woods and swamps, and a deluge of rain, whilst we recounted the legends and ghost-stories, with which the Scottish crones are wont to affright their juvenile audience on that dreaded night . . . [36]

Possibly the first Halloween story for children published in book form came in 1888: 'Elsie's Hallowe'en Experience' (from a collection also bearing that title) by Mary D. Brine. It tells of Elsie, a little girl experiencing her first Halloween, and includes this revealing description of Halloween by Elsie's mother:

> It is the vigil of Hallowmas, or 'All Saints' Day', dear, and is a relic of pagan times, when people were given to superstitious, heathenish ideas and notions, and were great believers in mysterious rites and ceremonies. The Scotch people of old times kept to the custom of celebrating Hallowe'en, and fancied it to be a night when fairies were unusually active, and spirits walked about. In the north of England it is called 'nut-crack night.' There's really nothing in it at all, but like many of those queer ancient customs it hangs on as years go by, and has become a sort of institution now, as they call it, – a night devoted to fun and all sorts of frolic, as your little friends will probably show you.[37]

The dismissive tone expressed by Elsie's mother soon vanished from the pages of fiction as Halloween grew in popularity and entered the twentieth century. Compare it to 1915's *Ethel Morton's Holidays*, in which Halloween is now a popular civic celebration, with clubs and committees hosting parties (and boys shamefacedly admitting to past pranking, but promising not to indulge this year). *Halloween at Merryvale* of 1916 begins with a definition of the word 'Halloween' itself, but Halloween activities require no explanation in this charming tale of a boys' party, hosted by mother dressed as a witch and father dressed as a ghost, and consisting of bobbing for apples, snap-apple, retrieving a dime from a pan of flour using only the mouth, and receiving gifts of fake spiders and snakes (since these are boys, after all). By 1941, printing techniques had improved enough to allow for colour illustrations on every page of the early reader *Jack O' Lantern Twins*, but the Halloween activities are strangely similar: there's still no mention of trick or treat, but children have a party in which they bob for apples, play other games

Illustration by
Charles F. Lester
from *Hallowe'en
at Merryvale*,
showing a boys'
Halloween party,
1926.

The boys screamed with laughter as the queer-looking things
bumped about on the table.

and have a decorative dinner. The only difference between this party
and *Halloween at Merryvale*'s is that the children arrive in costumes
and masks.

There were surprisingly few Halloween books for children published in the 1940s and '50s; *Georgie's Halloween* by Robert Bright,
from 1958, is the best-known from this time. It offers a gentle tale of
a shy ghost who becomes popular on Halloween, and is still fondly
remembered by many adults.

It probably took the book version of the very successful television
special *It's the Great Pumpkin, Charlie Brown* to create the demand
for more children's Halloween books. *It's the Great Pumpkin, Charlie*

Brown was first printed in 1967, and was reprinted a year later in mass market paperback; within a few years, the popularity of children's Halloween books had blossomed, and dozens were printed during the 1970s, leading to hundreds and thousands in the succeeding decades. Now there are Halloween books for children of every possible type: non-fiction histories, crafts guides, pop-up books, sticker books, scratch-and-sniff books and of course storybooks are published every year.

In 1998, as the young adult fiction area was just starting to expand, a previously unknown author named J. K. Rowling introduced the world to a boy wizard called Harry Potter, and a new Halloween favourite was born. The seven books (not counting peripheral volumes) in the phenomenally successful *Harry Potter* series have made clever use of Halloween, with scenes of Halloween celebrations that include live decorations (bats), huge pumpkins grown specifically for the day by Hagrid, and real ghosts as guests. The Potter books have spawned a new wealth of Halloween costumes and collectibles, but it's also possible to suggest that the books owe part of their success to Halloween's expanding popularity in the late 1990s. Perhaps both point to a search for magic and fantasy in the life of the modern urban dweller.

Halloween in Hollywood

Surprisingly, Hollywood was late to the Halloween party. Prior to 1944, there were no significant uses of Halloween in feature films, and only a handful of animated shorts that had used it; the most well-known of these is the almost surreal 'Betty Boop's Hallowe'en Party' of 1933, which includes such images as a pranking gorilla chalking an owl and finally being chased by witch decorations come to life. Radio, however, was still the dominant medium of broadcasting and discovered the charms of the festival early on. Halloween-themed radio plays were airing as early as 1933, when the horror series *The Witch's Tale* broadcast a show entitled 'All Hallows' Eve'. Nearly every suspense or horror programme (*Inner*

Sanctum, Suspense, Quiet, Please) over the next twenty years featured at least one Halloween episode, but the day was also featured on comedy and variety series, including *The Jack Benny Program* – which made jokes about pranking, costumes and food – and *The Edgar Bergen and Charlie McCarthy Show*, which featured special guest Orson Welles.

Welles had, in 1938, created not only the most famous Halloween radio special in history, but also the greatest Halloween prank ever when he broadcast his adaptation of H. G. Wells's classic science fiction story *The War of the Worlds*. Aired as a one-hour teleplay over the Columbia Broadcasting System on 30 October 1938, the Mercury Theatre production presented such a realistic performance that over a million listeners phoned police stations, convinced a Martian attack was taking place. At the end of the show, Welles reminded his audience that 'it's Halloween', and the next day the 21-year-old held a press conference about the uproar created by his broadcast. The controversy continued for some time, with the FCC taking a dim view of fictitious news broadcasts afterward, while Adolf Hitler delivered a speech in which he referred to the broadcast as evidence of democracy's corruption and decadence. Both praised and damned, there were two incontrovertible facts about *The War of the Worlds*: it made a star of Orson Welles, and it became a Halloween classic, still broadcast by radio stations every year. As radio expert Richard J. Hand has noted, 'it remains unlikely that any Halloween "trick or treat" will match the sheer audacity and tangible impact of this 1938 offering.'[38]

By the 1950s, radio had been pushed aside by the new medium of television, and Halloween found an equally warm welcome there. As with radio, Halloween could be found in nearly all types of television shows, and often painted an interesting light on each decade's interpretation of the day. In 1952, for instance, the hit sitcom *The Adventures of Ozzie and Harriet* aired an episode entitled 'Halloween Party' which centred on Ozzie's misguided attempt to stage a gathering, but also featured trick or treat heavily. Youngest son Ricky is excited about going out, but Harriet seems surprised by his shop-bought skeleton costume; later, when two small children come to the door, their trick or treat outfits consist of ordinary clothing with simple face paint. Ozzie also mentions several times his belief that Halloween is really for children, although the adults are planning their own party.

A decade and a half later, Halloween was more popular than ever, and trick or treat was well-established, as evidenced by sitcoms like *Bewitched*, a series about the comedic adventures of a real witch trying to fit into suburban life. In an episode from 1967 called 'The Safe and Sane Halloween', trick or treat is taken for granted, and dozens of children are depicted prowling the neighbourhood in a variety of costumes. Even the science fiction series *Star Trek* had a Halloween episode: in 1967 they broadcast 'Catspaw', written by famed horror author Robert Bloch, the creator of *Psycho* and author of 'The Cloak'. The story focuses on two mysterious aliens who have created a world based on the human subconscious, and both Halloween and trick or treat are referenced.

In 1989 and 1990, two successful comedies aired episodes that would return such high ratings and critical acclaim that they begat yearly Halloween specials: *Roseanne* ran the episode 'Boo!', and *The*

Costume-less trick-or-treaters from 1952's *The Adventures of Ozzie and Harriet.*

Simpsons began their 'Treehouse of Horror' cycle. *The Simpsons* played primarily on Halloween's relationship to horror movies and literature, and even included a parody of Poe's classic poem 'The Raven' with father Homer as the narrator beset by a raven bearing son Bart's features. More interesting, in a way, is 'Boo!', which depicted the working-class family at the heart of *Roseanne* creating a home haunt (a 'Tunnel of Terror' through their house, complete with set dressing and grotesque makeup), limning a moment somewhere in between the old-style 'Trails of Terror' and the high-tech haunts that would soon mark American Halloweens.

Shows that are already part of the horror genre have often playfully inverted Halloween, creating highly regarded episodes in the process. In 1997, *Buffy the Vampire Slayer* presented the first (and most successful) of three Halloween episodes with 'Halloween', which began with the notion that Halloween was the dullest night of the year for the eponymous teenaged slayer, and moved on to reveal that enchanted costumes were turning their wearers into the actual characters they represented. Unfortunately, Buffy had chosen to dress as an eighteenth-century lady and proved capable of little more than fainting at the sight of demonic creatures.

The *Buffy* spin-off series *Angel* offered a playful Halloween episode in 2003, 'Life of the Party', which suggested that demons and creatures enjoyed a good Halloween party as much as any human. And the 2011 season finale of HBO's *True Blood* featured Wiccans using Samhain to call on the help of ancestors to protect them not from the show's vampires, but from other Wiccans. The show apparently resulted in a rise of youthful interest in Wicca: 'Since the new season of "True Blood" began, I've seen an increase in new members who are in their teens', reported an Atlanta witch who runs an online pagan forum.[39] Unfortunately, the season finale left many of its Wiccan viewers less than amused by the actions of its witch characters, which included mispronouncing 'Samhain' as 'Sam-a-hayne'.

While Halloween was playing out on radios and televisions throughout the twentieth and twenty-first centuries and cross-pollinating the actual celebration by giving rise to hundreds of costumes, depictions of it seemed to be strangely absent from the movie arena. In fact, it took the releases of *Meet Me in St Louis* and *Arsenic and Old Lace* in 1944 to solidly introduce Halloween to moviegoers for the first time. Vincente Minnelli's part-drama part-musical may be chiefly remembered today for the performance of a young Judy Garland and 'The Trolley Song', but *Meet Me in St Louis* also features an extended look at an idealized Halloween of 1903, complete with pranking children and bonfires.

More interesting, though, is Frank Capra's *Arsenic and Old Lace*. The film opens with Halloween-themed credits and informs us up front that the date is Halloween, and also features a group of costumed children (who never utter 'trick or treat') being given treats, despite the fact that the Broadway play upon which the movie was based was set in September. Obviously Halloween was popular enough by 1944 that the film's producers opted to centre the action on that day, and *Arsenic and Old Lace* remains a favourite family movie for Halloween viewing.

Over the next decade, the two best portrayals of Halloween on film both came from the Disney Studios. In 1952, their animated short 'Trick or Treat' confirmed that the masked solicitation ritual had finally been completely integrated into American society. The short focuses on Donald Duck's three trick or treating nephews, and the pranks the irascible Donald plays on them until a friendly witch places him under a spell. More telling, though was the 1949 release of *The Adventures of Ichabod and Mr Toad*, a feature comprised of two adaptations: *The Wind and the Willows* and *The Legend of Sleepy Hollow*. Narrated by Bing Crosby and overall sticking fairly closely to Washington Irving's original story, the Disney version is notable for changing the tale's setting from simply 'autumn' to very specifically Halloween. In the original tale, Ichabod is invited to 'a merry-making or "quilting frolic"',[40] but in the Disney adaptation he is not only invited to a Halloween party, but a party at which (as the narrator informs us), 'Van Tassel always called upon his guests to tell him ghostly tales of Halloween'. There's even a song, entitled 'The Headless Horseman', performed by Crosby, which tells us that the title character is 'a fright, on Halloween night'. The Disney film was so successful in firmly enmeshing Irving's tale and Halloween that most readers will probably be surprised to discover that the original story makes no mention of the festival.

For the next 50 years, Halloween cinema was dominated by John Carpenter and his seminal slasher *Halloween* (1979). The film's original title – as conceived by producer Irwin Yablans – was *The Babysitter Murders*, but the canny move to change the title was undoubtedly a huge part of the film's success (and successful it was – its investment of $300,000 earned back over 50 times that). Yablans also compared *Halloween* to horror radio: 'I grew up with radio, *Inner Sanctum*, *Lights Out*, radio horror shows . . . and I said I want it to be like a radio show. I want it to be spooky, scary, but leave much of it to the audience.'[41]

Halloween none the less gave audiences plenty of sexually fuelled violence and (implied) gore in keeping with the new explicitness of the 1970s, and was an immediate surprise hit. It also scored with critics: Roger Ebert gave the film four stars and noted, '*Halloween* is an absolutely merciless thriller . . . If you don't want to have a really terrifying experience, don't see *Halloween*.'[42] Genre movie expert Kim Newman praised the film's 'eerie jack-o'-lantern mood', and suggested that *Halloween* started the first exploitation cinema trend to deal primarily with women.[43] And slasher scholar Adam Rockoff, in his comprehensive overview *Going to Pieces*, had this to say:

> It is difficult to overestimate the importance of *Halloween*. Many of the conventions which have become staples of the slasher – the subjective camera, the Final Girl, the significant date setting – were either pioneered or perfected in the film.[44]

There were occasional mentions of Halloween inserted into other films during the 1970s – most curiously, perhaps, in William Friedkin's adaptation of William Peter Blatty's *The Exorcist* (1973), which includes one unexplained shot of laughing trick or treaters rushing past the camera – but it took Carpenter's film to prove just how effective using Halloween extensively could be, and other films

Japanese programme book cover for *Halloween*.

began to follow suit. Surely one of the oddest Halloween films (and one of the oddest sequels) ever was 1982's *Halloween III: Season of the Witch,* which completely dispensed with the character of masked killer Michael Myers and focused instead on a mysterious Irish mask manufacturer named Conal Cochran (played by Dan O'Herlihy).

Cochran, as it turns out, is actually an ancient Celt who intends to offer up America's children on 31 October as a huge Samhain sacrifice, and the film's finale implies that he has succeeded. *Halloween III* is probably notable today only for being the first horror movie to focus on Samhain.

Another film in 1982 certainly enjoyed far more box-office success, and made fine use of Halloween: Steven Spielberg's *E.T.: The Extra-Terrestrial*. Much of the film's action takes place on Halloween, and Spielberg ably uses the day to help set a tone of magic and wonder. *E.T.* not only became one of the most beloved films of all time but even transformed an existing candy into a new Halloween favourite: Reese's Pieces, small bite-sized candies with a peanut butter-flavoured interior that the young hero Elliott feeds to the diminutive alien at one point.

One of the few mentions of Halloween in the entire body of Stephen King's work appeared in the film *Silver Bullet* (1985), which had a screenplay adapted by King from his book *Cycle of the Werewolf* and included a significant change from the book: a werewolf slaying that had been set on New Year's Eve was moved to Halloween for the film version. Hollywood, it seems, is always ready to capitalize on Halloween, especially considering its rising global popularity. King, on the other hand, has made little use of it otherwise, with only a few brief mentions appearing in works such as the short story 'Jerusalem's Lot' and the final volume of the *Dark Tower* series.

It wasn't until 1993, however, that Halloween was finally awarded what many fans consider the ultimate Halloween movie: Tim Burton's stop-motion animated *The Nightmare Before Christmas*. If Carpenter's *Halloween* had given the festival licence to explore its sinister side sixteen years earlier, *Nightmare* returned some of the sense of magic to 31 October. Burton first sketched the idea out as a poem while he was working as an animator at Disney; then, in 1990, after he'd directed two hit films (*Batman* and *Edward Scissorhands*), Disney agreed to finance a feature film. Burton, who had also designed the characters, decided on stop-motion animation as the best way of bringing his drawings to life, and he hired animator

Henry Selick to direct; he also worked out the film's songs and basic story with composer Danny Elfman before turning over the screenwriting to Caroline Thompson. *Nightmare* is the story of Jack Skellington, the elegant Pumpkin King of Halloweentown, who stumbles on Christmas one day and tries to recreate Halloween in its image. Burton, who grew up in the quiet Los Angeles suburb of Burbank, has had a lifelong love affair with holidays and festivals, especially Halloween:

> when you grow up in a blank environment, any form of ritual, like a holiday, gives you a sense of place . . . [holidays] were very much a grounding or a way to experience seasons, because in California you don't get any. So at least you could walk in the supermarket aisles and see the Halloween display and the fall leaves . . . To me, Halloween has always been the most fun night of the year. It's where rules are dropped and you can be anything at all. Fantasy rules. It's only scary in a funny way. Nobody's out to really scare anybody else to death. They're out to delight people with their scariness, which is what Halloween is all about and what *Nightmare* is all about.[45]

Indeed, *The Nightmare Before Christmas* is appealing thanks to both its good-natured tone and its design, which perfectly encapsulates Halloween and horror iconography, albeit in a playful way. The film spawned a torrent of merchandising, and collectors snapped up everything from action figures to limited-edition ceramic recreations of scenes from the film. In fact, *Nightmare*'s merchandising remains one of the few cases in which initial demand actually exceeded the amount of available material. Although the film achieved only minor box office success on its original u.s. theatrical release, foreign releases (especially in Japan) and American re-releases – including a 3D release in 2006 and 'Sing-Along' releases in which the audience is encouraged to accompany the onscreen songs – have proven popular since. The film scored with critics: Roger Ebert weighed in positively again, calling it 'a feast for the eyes and the imagination'.[46] *Time* magazine critic Richard Corliss noted (with inadvertent irony, perhaps, given Halloween's coming move into other global cultures), '*Nightmare* can be viewed as a parable of cultural imperialism, of the futility of imposing one's entertainment values on another society.'[47]

The Nightmare Before Christmas also spun off in one other interesting direction: in 2001, Disneyland redressed the Haunted Mansion attraction with *Nightmare* characters for the Halloween/Christmas season, calling it 'Haunted Mansion Holiday'. The remodelled ride, which featured characters from the film (including Jack Skellington, Sally and the ghost dog Zero) and a new original soundtrack, was such a hit that it became a yearly attraction. It has even given rise to 'Haunted Mansion Holiday' merchandise sold throughout the park.

One other film released directly to DVD in 2009 after Warner Bros opted not to release it theatrically found favour with both horror and Halloween fans: Michael Dougherty's *Trick 'r Treat* took the form of a 1970s-era anthology film, interweaving four stories set in a small town on Halloween night. The film incorporates many of the key elements of the modern Halloween celebration, including (of course) trick or treat, costume parties, urban legends, jack-o'-lantern carving and yard decorating, and was praised by such reviewers as *Variety*'s Joe Leydon, who suggested it would become a 'Halloween perennial'.[48] Although darker (the film was rated 'R' in the USA) and bloodier than *The Nightmare Before Christmas*, *Trick 'r Treat* was popular with many of the fans of that film for capturing Halloween in both its art direction and storyline. One horror film website raved that it 'feels not just like a series of independent stories set on Halloween, but a complete picture of what makes this holiday so beloved, so dangerous, and so much damn fun . . . an instant Halloween classic'.[49]

The Art of Halloween

Given how Halloween lovers respond to the festival's visual tropes, it's perhaps surprising that Halloween has seldom appeared in either the fine arts or the more recent venue of graphic novels. A wealth of nineteenth-century engravings from books and magazines notwithstanding, Halloween's appearances in the world of fine art were few, most notable being Daniel Maclise's *Snap-apple Night* of 1833, and several works by the quintessential American painter Norman Rockwell, especially his *Saturday Evening Post* cover of 1920 showing a young girl draped in a sheet and holding up a jack-o'-lantern while an older man in a business suit reacts in exaggerated shock. Halloween has been more popular with the latest generation of pop artists, who have gathered together for an annual exhibit of Halloween art in Chicago, and have also created online galleries at such websites as halloweenartexhibit.com. Petaluma, a small town in Northern California, has been hosting the 'Halloween and Vine' Halloween art show since 1996. This juried art show also offers collectors the chance to buy original art ranging from paintings to dolls to surreal papier mâché figures, and takes place

Daniel Maclise, *Snap-apple Night*, 1833, oil on canvas.

Little Old Witch, a contemporary Halloween art figure by Scott Smith / Rucus Studio.

for only one day each year. Hundreds of collectors fly in for the show, coming to spend thousands of dollars each on the exclusive, one-of-a-kind works. These buyers frequently hold large collections of vintage Halloween memorabilia as well and cite both nostalgia and the company of fellow collectors as assets. 'There's a real camaraderie among all these people who love Halloween – they get it', notes Halloween artist Scott Smith of Rucus Studio.[50]

Graphic novel representations of Halloween have been limited almost exclusively to the lesser-known series and publishers, with one major exception: *Batman: The Long Halloween*, originally published in a series of thirteen comic books between 1996 and 1997. Sadly, despite the title, *The Long Halloween* makes very little use of the day itself, focusing instead on a mysterious killer named 'Holiday'. The lack of Halloween references in other superhero comics might suggest that a festival in which wearing a costume as a form of empowerment has no place in a genre wherein costumes are routinely linked to characters who are already powerful.

More appropriate was a three-book series put out by Tokyopop called *I Luv Halloween* which was released in three volumes from 2005 to 2007 and collected into an 'Ultimate Edition' in one volume in 2008. Written by Keith Giffen with art by Benjamin Roman, this English-language manga series chronicles the adventures of pre-adolescent trick or treaters who take on zombies, aliens and a murderous baby sister while trying to trick or treat; it pokes irreverent fun at Halloween, and was described by *Publisher's Weekly* as a 'black comedy that reads as if Quentin Tarantino and Tim Burton had collaborated on a Halloween heist story'.[51] Tokyopop and Menfond Electronic Arts also created a series of animated online shorts based on *I Luv Halloween*.

If Halloween has languished in some art forms, such is certainly not the case with folk art. Although the term 'folk art' can be difficult to define, it typically refers to work by untrained, non-professional artists; it is usually distinguished from crafts, in which the creator follows pre-existing instructions, and should also not include deliberate reproductions of existing work. Folk art is also often regional, although the Internet has given folk artists a worldwide

Contemporary Halloween yard decorations.

venue in which to display and sell their goods through collective sites like ebay or etsy.com, or through smaller or personal websites. Traditional, vintage Halloween folk art is rare, considering that much of it was produced from cheap materials and was intended only for seasonal use; true folk art may also take the form of what folklorist Jack Santino calls *assemblage*, essentially a yard display of carefully grouped items like scarecrows or harvest figures, jack-o'-lanterns,

HALLOWEEN AND POPULAR CULTURE

other seasonal harvest byproducts like hay bales or Indian corn, and paper decorations and hanging ghosts. Pamela Apkarian-Russell's Castle Halloween Museum includes a wing dedicated to folk art, with an emphasis on specific artists like Bethany Lowe and Debbee Thibault and on the peculiar medium of Southern face jugs, large ceramic jugs modelled to look like ghastly faces.

Monster Mashes and Thrillers: Halloween Music

Halloween may not have a standard repertoire of carols à la Christmas, but music has been associated with the festival throughout its history. In the distant past, souling was often performed with songs, and sometimes the soulers were accompanied by musicians. A description from 1910 notes:

> Three middle-aged men; with a concertina, have just been souling here. They began well but ended with very bad verses about ale and strong beer which, they said, was all of which they came.[52]

That same report noted that the melody was 'undoubtedly pre-Reformation and is cast in the style of the church music of the period'.[53] In 1886 a correspondent from Chester described the souling song as being nearly identical to 'part of a march of which Handel claimed the authorship', and even suggested that Handel had taken his work from the souling song.[54] For the most part, the souling songs were delivered by children rather than adults. The Grülacks, guisers who visited houses in Shetland at Halloween, were sometimes accompanied by a fiddler who played while they danced with the girls in the household, and the Manx sang the traditional 'Hop-tu-naa' ballad at Halloween. Music was central to both Irish and Scottish Halloween celebrations, which usually ended with dancing. One description of a nineteenth-century Irish Halloween party notes that the musical performances were the climax of the evening:

At last came the crowning delight of the evening, the Halloween jig. This was a reel in which everyone joined, and there
was nothing short of ecstasy in the tumult of stamping feet,
snapping fingers, happy laughter, mingling with the wild
music of Larry O'Hara's pipes, and the frantic screams – for
they were nothing else – from the fiddle of the great musician,
One-eyed Murtagh.[55]

Somehow the music didn't export to American Halloween celebrations, and there's little mention of singing or dancing in connection
with nineteenth-century parties in the US (although these do also
seem to have been mainly held for children). By the early twentieth
century, popular music did offer up a few seasonal songs, bearing
titles like 'Jack O' Lantern Rag' and 'Hallowe'en Frolic'; today, these
songs are remembered more for the beguiling graphics on their sheet
music than for their musical qualities. The Halloween party guides
of the 1920s and '30s often created Halloween songs intended to
be sung to existing tunes – 'On Halloween', for example, was set to
'Yankee Doodle Dandy' and included this chorus:

> Goodness gracious, how we ran!
> Goodness gracious, granny;
> I never knew that clumsy boys
> With feet could be so handy.[56]

Later in the century, Halloween music consisted mostly of any
horror or science fiction-themed popular song ('Witch Doctor', 'I
Put a Spell on You', and 'Purple People Eater' have all been favourites) until 1962, when a novelty song by an unsuccessful actor hit
#1 on the Billboard charts and virtually became Halloween's official
anthem: 'Monster Mash' by Bobby 'Boris' Pickett and the Crypt-
kicker Five. Inspired in equal part by the 'Monster Culture' of the
early 1960s and the 'Mashed Potato' dance craze (which was set off
by Dee Dee Sharp's hit 'Mashed Potato Time' of 1962), 'Monster
Mash' tells the story – in Pickett's droll impression of Boris Karloff
– of a mad scientist whose creation leads an army of monsters in

a new dance sensation. The song spent two weeks in October 1962 atop the Billboard charts, and became a perennial Halloween favourite, later covered by artist ranging from Mannheim Steamroller to The Smashing Pumpkins to Karloff himself, in a performance on the music show *Shindig* in 1965.

In 1983, 'Monster Mash' was nearly dethroned by the song behind a fourteen-minute-long music video: Michael Jackson's 'Thriller'. The video, which was directed by John Landis and features Jackson dancing with legions of zombies after turning into one himself, is considered the most influential music video ever made, the first time the then-nascent form of music video was really married to the short film; but 'Thriller' – both the song and the video – became equally well-known as a new Halloween favourite. 'Thriller' is an ode to horror movies, and the irresistible combination of music and monsters was tailor-made for Halloween. 'Thriller' not only found the top spot on Halloween party mix tapes, it also became a costume favourite (Jackson's distinctive red jacket from the video was copied endlessly) and dance groups still perform the video's choreography in Halloween parades every year. Even in Ukraine's largest city, Kiev, where pumpkins are associated more with a tradition of turning down suitors than making jack-o'-lanterns, Halloween has been celebrated by masses of 'Thriller' fans performing the dance moves on a main street, with videos of the event appearing shortly thereafter on such websites as YouTube.[57]

The most recent major contribution to the library of Halloween music comes from *The Nightmare Before Christmas*. The first major song presented in Tim Burton's film is 'This is Halloween', composed by Danny Elfman and describing how the ghoulish residents of Halloweentown view their holiday. 'This is Halloween' was also made popular in a cover version by Marilyn Manson.

Halloween Culture

Manson, in his persona as a Goth rocker, ultimately raises the question of whether Halloween has influenced Goth style and music. And in what other ways has it fed into popular culture, rather than vice versa? Halloween expert Lesley Bannatyne refers to the recent cross-pollination of counter-culture movements with Halloween as the 'Halloweening of America',[58] and suggests that everything from the rise of interest in paranormal investigations over the last ten years to Goth music and fashion to the nationwide fascination with zombies has arisen partly out of Halloween, rather than the other way around.

Horror film scholars have suggested that horror proliferates during conservative political administrations – consider the rise of giant mutant films during the 1950s, or slasher movies during the Reagan era. Is it a coincidence, then, that Halloween's popularity exploded during the first decade of the twenty-first century, when George W. Bush was in office? Now, with divisive politics and an uncertain economy looming over the American landscape, Halloween is becoming both more openly horrific, with increasingly violent and realistic haunted attractions, and extending its influence, both around the globe and throughout the year. In 2011, there were haunted attractions opened on other festivals – Sinister Pointe in Brea, California, for example, now offers themed hauntings at Christmas and Valentine's Day – and there is a trend toward year-round haunted attractions. In discussing the increasing length of time these attractions are staying open to accommodate consumer demand, the president of a haunters' association calls haunted attractions a 'subculture movement',[59] a description that could almost be applied to Halloween in general.

Aggressive retailing may have started the globalization of Halloween, but in many areas – South Africa, Russia, Hong Kong – it's been embraced equally by subcultures who see it as a form of artistic expression. Raves, sports events, makeup schools, costumers, organic growers and social networks have all helped disseminate Halloween culture around the world. The festival's visual motifs – grinning jack-o'-lanterns and skeletal faces – have been integrated and re-purposed into everything from mall decorations to region-specific greeting cards.

Halloween has endured centuries of political and religious criticism, economic downturns, real terror and attempts to ban it even

1912 postcard.

as it's been adopted by new generations and movements. It has repeatedly been resurrected and modified to be celebrated anew, and it is now enjoyed by much of the world. The celebration's playful use of frightening ideas and images seems to hold an appeal that transcends nations and eras, and that speaks of a universal human need to mock and transform death and darkness – even as winter approaches.

References

1 Halloween: The Misunderstood Festival

1 Charles Vallancey, *Collectanea de Rebus Hibernicis* (Dublin, 1786), vol. III, pp. 443–4.

2 Sir William Jones to the Second Earl Spencer, 10 September 1787, in *Letters of Sir William Jones*, ed. G. Cannon (Oxford, 1970), vol. II, pp. 768–9.

3 Ralph and Adelin Linton, *Halloween Through Twenty Centuries* (New York, 1950), p. 4.

4 Bishop Kyrill of Seattle, 'On Halloween', *Orthodox Life*, XLIII/5 (1993), online at www.holycross-hermitage.com, last accessed 7 March 2012.

5 'Art. VIII. – Greenland, the adjacent Seas, and the North-West Passage to the Pacific Ocean; illustrated in a Voyage to Davis's Strait during the Summer of 1817', *London Quarterly Review*, XIX (April 1818), p. 213.

6 'Hallow', *Oxford English Dictionary*, online version (2011), at www.oed.com, last accessed 7 March 2012.

7 Richard Polwhele, *Historical Views of Devonshire* (Exeter, 1793), vol. I, p. 29.

8 W. Hutchinson, *A View of Northumberland with an Excursion to the Abbey of Mailross in Scotland* (Newcastle, 1776), vol. II, p.18.

9 Robert Haven Schauffler, *Hallowe'en (Our American Holidays)* (New York, 1935), p. ix.

10 Ibid., p. x.

11 Whitley Stokes, ed., *The Martyrology of Oengus the Culdee* (London, 1905), p. 232.

12 John Brand, *Observations on Popular Antiquities* (London, 1813), vol. I, p. 309.

13 James A. H. Murray, ed., *A New English Dictionary on Historical Principles* (Oxford, 1888), vol. I, p. 234.

14 W. Harpley, ed., *Report and Transactions of the Devonshire Association for the Advancement of Science, Literature, and Art* (Plymouth, 1892), vol. XXVI, p. 297.

15 Brand, *Observations on Popular Antiquities*, p. 311.

16 John Stow, *A Survey of London* (London, 1598), p. 252.

17 Heinrich Kramer and Jacob Sprenger, *Malleus Maleficarum* (New York, 2007), p. 41.

18 Brand, *Observations on Popular Antiquities*, p. 311.

19 'Ancient Scottish Life', *Littell's Living Age*, vol. X (1846), p. 371.

20 'Should Christians Participate in Halloween?', at www.christiananswers.net, last accessed 7 March 2012.

21 P. H. Ditchfield, *Old English Sports: Pastimes and Customs* (London, 1891), p. 108.

22 Brand, *Observations on Popular Antiquities*, p. 313.

23 R. H. Whitelocke, ed., *Memoirs, Biographical and Historical, of Bulstrode Whitelocke* (London, 1860), p. 57.

24 Jesse Salisbury, *A Glossary of Words and Phrases used in S.E. Worcestershire* (London, 1893), p. 66.

2 Snap-apple Night and November Eve: Halloween in the British Isles

1 James Cranstoun, ed., *The Poems of Alexander Montgomerie* (Edinburgh and London, 1887), p. 69.

2 Sir Walter Scott, *Minstrelsy of the Scottish Border* (Kelso, 1802), vol. I, pp. lxxv–viii.

3 Sir Walter Scott, *The Monastery* (London and New York, 1896), p. 28.

4 Sir Walter Scott, *Waverley; or, 'Tis Sixty Years Since* (Edinburgh, 1814), vol. I, p. 189.

5 Robert Jamieson, *Popular Ballads and Songs, from Tradition, Manuscripts, and Scarce Editions* (Edinburgh, 1806), vol. II, pp. 187–90.

6 Thomas Hardy, *The Return of the Native* (New York, 1917), p. 15.

7 David Brown, 'All-Hallow Eve Myths', *St. Nicholas: An Illustrated Magazine for Young Folks*, IX/1 (1881), p. 23.

8 Thomas Pennant, *A Tour in Scotland Part II* (London, 1772), p. 47.

9 Jack Santino, *The Hallowed Eve: Dimensions of Culture in a Calendar Festival in Northern Ireland* (Lexington, 1998), p. 90.

10 John Harland and T. T. Wilkinson, *Lancashire Folk-lore: Illustrative of the Superstitious Beliefs and Practices, Local Customs and Usages of the People of the County Palatine* (London, 1867), p. 211.

11 Lachlan Shaw, *The History of the Province of Moray* (Elgin, 1827), p. 283.

12 William Hone, *The Every-Day Book; or, the Guide to the Year* (London, 1825), p. 1412.

13 James Napier, *Folk Lore: Or, Superstitious Beliefs in the West of Scotland Within This Century* (Paisley, 1879), pp. 179–80.

14 Robert Burns, *Poems, Chiefly in the Scottish Dialect* (Kilmarnock, 1786), pp. 101–17.

15 John Gay, *The Shepherd's Week* (London, 1721), pp. 34–5.

16 Ibid.

17 John Gregorson Campbell, *Witchcraft and Second Sight in the Highlands and Islands of Scotland* (Glasgow, 1902), pp. 285–6.

18 Lady Wilde, *Ancient Legends, Mystic Charms, and Superstitions of Ireland* (Boston, MA, 1888), p. 110.

19 Burns, *Poems*, p. 110.

20 Napier, *Folk Lore*, p. 59.

21 William Sharp, 'Halloween: A Threefold Chronicle', *Harper's New Monthly Magazine*, LXXIII (1886), pp. 854–6.

22 Charles Kirkpatrick Sharpe, *A Historical Account of the Belief in Witchcraft in Scotland* (London, 1884), p. 97.

23 Hone, *The Every-Day Book*, p. 1414.

24 Anne Beale, *Traits and Stories of the Welsh Peasantry* (London, 1849), p. 75.

25 'Legends Respecting Trees', *Chambers's Edinburgh Journal*, vol. I (1844), p. 189.

26 John Brand, *Observations on Popular Antiquities* (London, 1810), p. 380.

27 William S. Walsh, *Curiosities of Popular Customs and of Rites, Ceremonies, Observances, and Miscellaneous Antiquities,* (Philadelphia, PA, 1898), p. 507.

28 W. T. Kenyon, 'Malpas: All Saints' Day, 1880', *Cheshire Sheaf*, II (1880), pp. 185–6.

29 Joseph Train, *An Historical and Statistical Account of the Isle of Man, from the Earliest Times to the Present Date; With a View of Its Ancient Laws, Peculiar Customs, and Popular Superstitions* (Douglas, Isle of Man, 1845), vol. II, p. 123.

30 Doug Sandle, 'Hop TuNaa, My Father's Gone Away – A Personal and Cultural Account of the Manx Halloween', in *Treat or Trick?*

Halloween in a Globalising World, ed. Malcolm Foley and Hugh O'Donnell (Newcastle upon Tyne, 2009), p. 94.

31 C. W. Empson, 'Weather Proverbs and Sayings Not Contained in Inwards' or Swainsons' Books', *Folk-lore Record*, IV (1881), p. 128.

32 A. R. Wright, *British Calendar Customs: England*: vol. III: *Fixed Festivals, June–December, Inclusive*, ed. T. E. Lones (London, 1940), p. 135.

33 Robert Fergusson, *The Works of Robert Fergusson; with a Short Account of His Life, and a Concise Glossary* (Edinburgh, 1805), pp. 137–8.

34 Rev. Alfred Povah, *The Annals of the Parishes of St Olave Hart Street and Allhallows Staining, in the City of London* (London, 1894), p. 315.

35 Finlo Rohrer, 'The Transatlantic Halloween Divide', *BBC News Magazine*, 29 October 2010), at www.bbc.co.uk/news/magazine, last accessed 9 March 2012.

36 Ibid.

37 Andrea Felsted and Esther Bintliff, 'Halloween Spawns Monster High Street Sales', *Financial Times*, 31 October 2009, at www.ft.com, last accessed 9 March 2012.

3 Trick or Treat in the New World

1 'Hallowe'en at Balmoral Castle', in *A Hallowe'en Anthology: Literary and Historical Writings Over the Centuries*, ed. Lisa Morton (Jefferson, NC, 2008), p. 42.

2 Elizabeth A. Irwin, 'A Witches' Revel for Hallowe'en', *Good Housekeeping*, XLVII (1908), p. 393.

3 Iona and Peter Opie, *The Lore and Language of Schoolchildren* (New York, 2000), p. 268.

4 Martha Russell Orne, *Hallowe'en: How to Celebrate It* (New York, 1898), p. 27.

5 Emma Woodman, 'Hallowe'en', in *The School Arts Book*, ed. Henry Turner Bailey (Worcester, MA, 1906), vol. V, p. 146.

6 Mary E. Blain, *Games for Hallowe'en* (New York, 1912), p. 9.

7 George J. Cowan, *Window Backgrounds: A Collection of Drawings and Descriptions of Store Window Backgrounds* (Chicago, IL, 1912), p. 133.

8 A. J. Edgell, 'All Hallowe'en Window Displays', *The Jewelers' Circular-Weekly*, LXXVI (1918), p. 103.

9 A. Neely Hall, *The Boy Craftsman: Practical and Profitable Ideas for a Boy's Leisure Hours* (Boston, MA, 1905), pp. 281–2.

10 Lenore K. Dolan, *The Best Halloween Book* (Chicago, IL, 1931), p. 30.

11 'Pie Versus the Prankster', *The Rotarian*, LV/4 (1939), pp. 50–51.

12 'Halloween Pranks Keep Police on Hop', in *The Halloween Catalog Collection: 55 Catalogs from the Golden Age of Halloween*, ed. Ben Truwe (Medford, OR, 2003), p. xvii.

13 Doris Hudson Moss, 'A Victim of the Window-Soaping Brigade?', *The American Home*, XXII (1939), p. 48.

14 Kenneth Hein, 'Private Label Halloween Candy Sales Frightful', *Adweek*, 15 October 2009, at www.adweek.com, last accessed 9 March 2012.

15 Ibid..

16 Carl B. Holmberg, 'Things That Go *Snap-Rattle-Clang-Toot-Crank* in the Night: Halloween Noisemakers', in *Halloween and Other Festivals of Death and Life*, ed. Jack Santino (Knoxville, TN, 1994), pp. 221–46.

17 William Smith, *The History and Antiquities of Morley, in the West Riding of the County of York* (London, 1876), p. 92.

18 Maria Choi, 'Trick or Treat for UNICEF 60th Anniversary', UNICEF USA (2011), at http://inside.unicefusa.org, last accessed 9 March 2012.

19 David J. Skal, *The Monster Show: A Cultural History of Horror* (New York, 2001), revd edn, p. 266.

20 Tad Tuleja, 'Trick or Treat: Pre-Texts and Contexts', in *Halloween and Other Festivals of Death and Life*, ed. Santino, p. 94.

21 'Halloween Egg Sale Ban for Youths', *BBC News*, 17 October 2004, at http://news.bbc.co.uk, last accessed 9 March 2012.

22 Gregory Lee, 'A Darky's Halloween', in *Halloween Fun Book* (Chicago, IL, 1936), p. 28.

23 House of Representatives, Sixty-Seventh Congress, *The Ku-Klux Klan: Hearings Before the Committee on Rules* (Washington, DC, 1921), p. 131.

24 House Committee on Un-American Activities, *Activities of the Ku Klux Klan Organizations in the United States* (Washington, DC, 1965), p. 1775.

25 Charles Frederick White, 'Hallowe'en', in *Plea of the Negro Soldier and a Hundred Other Poems* (Easthampton, MA, 1908), pp. 93–4.

26 Jack Kugelmass, 'Wishes Come True: Designing the Greenwich Village Halloween Parade', in *Halloween and Other Festivals of Death and Life*, ed. Santino, p. 197.

27 'Fact Sheet 2011', *Village Halloween Parade* (2011), at www.halloween-nyc.com/press.php, last accessed 9 March 2012.

28 Lesley Pratt Bannatyne, *Halloween Nation: Behind the Scenes of America's Fright Night* (Gretna, LA, 2011), p. 60.

29 Rod Taylor, 'Trick or Drink?', *Promo Magazine*, 1 October 2003, at http://promomagazine.com, last accessed 9 March 2012.

30 Frances Somers, ed., *Minneapolis Hallowe'en Fun Book* (Minneapolis, MN, 1937), revd edn, p. 18.
31 Bannatyne, *Halloween Nation*, p. 165.
32 'Universal's Halloween Horror Nights', *The Official Clive Barker Resource – Revelations* (2001), at www.clivebarker.info, last accessed 9 March 2012.
33 Craig Wilson, 'Haunted Houses Get Really Scary', *USA Today*, 11 October 2006, at www.usatoday.com, last accessed 9 March 2012.
34 Ibid.
35 'Hauntworld Top 13 Haunted Houses 2010', at www.hauntworld. com (2010), accessed 9 March 2012.
36 Carrie Porter, 'Haunted House Proposed for Morton Grove', *MortonGrovePatch*, 10 May 2011, at http://mortongrove.patch.com, last accessed 9 March 2012.
37 New Destiny Christian Center, 'Hell House', at www.godestiny.org, last accessed 9 March 2012.
38 Barbara Mikkelson, 'Mall-O-Ween', *Snopes.com*, 14 March 2008, at www.snopes.com, last accessed 9 March 2012.
39 'Industry Statistics and Trends', *American Pet Products Association*, at www.americanpetproducts.org, last accessed 9 March 2012.
40 Stephanie Rosenbloom, 'Good Girls Go Bad, For a Day', *New York Times*, 19 October 2006, at www.nytimes.com, last accessed 9 March 2012.
41 Dr Gail Saltz, 'Sexy Little Devils? Policing Kids' Costumes', *Today*, 29 October 2008, at http://today.msnbc.msn.com, last accessed 9 March 2012.
42 NAMI, 'NAMI lists nation's worst "Halloween Horrors"', 28 October 2002, at http://www.nami.org, last accessed 9 March 2012.
43 Ibid.
44 John Ankerberg and John Weldon, *The Facts on Halloween: What Christians Need to Know* (Eugene, OR, 1996), pp. 7–8.
45 Douglas Stanglin, 'Vatican Warns Parents That Halloween is "Anti-Christian"', *USA Today*, 30 October 2009, at http://content.usatoday.com, last accessed 9 March 2012.
46 Tito Edwards, 'Vatican Condemnation of Halloween is False', *The American Catholic*, 31 October 2009, at http://the-american-catholic.com, last accessed 9 March 2012.
47 John Wildermuth, 'Los Altos Schools Ban Halloween / Costumes, Parties said to be "Religious Issues"', *SFGate.com*, 12 October 1995, at http://articles.sfgate.com, last accessed 9 March 2012.
48 Sue Shellenbarger, 'Saying Boo to Halloween', *The Wall Street*

Journal, 20 October 2010, at http://online.wsj.com, last accessed
9 March 2012.

49 Michael Woods, 'Births Decrease on Halloween, Study Finds',
TheStar.com, 30 October 2011, at www.thestar.com, last accessed
9 March 2012; Stephanie Newman, 'Is Halloween the New New
Year's?', *Psychology Today*, 26 October 2010, at www.psychologytoday.
com, last accessed 9 March 2012.

50 Jack Santino, 'Flexible Halloween: Longevity, Appropriation,
Multiplicity, and Contestation', in *Treat or Trick?: Halloween
in a Globalising World*, ed. Malcolm Foley and Hugh O'Donnell
(Newcastle upon Tyne, 2009), pp. 12–13.

4 *La Toussaint, Allerheiligen* and *Tutti i Santi*: The Global Celebration

1 Jonas Frykman, 'Tradition Without History', in *Treat or Trick?:
Halloween in a Globalising World*, ed. Malcolm Foley and Hugh
O'Donnell (Newcastle upon Tyne, 2009), page 131.

2 'The History of Halloween', at www.halloween-history.org, last
accessed 21 March 2012.

3 Agneta Lilja, 'Halloween' (2004), at www.sweden.se, last accessed
21 March 2012.

4 John Helsloot, 'The Fun of Fear: Performing Halloween in the
Netherlands', in *Treat or Trick?*, ed. Foley and O'Donnell, p. 160.

5 Editha Hörandner, 'Halloween. Ein Druidenfest oder die Liebe
zur Kontinuitat', in *Halloween in der Steiermark und anderswo*, ed.
Editha Hörandner (Berlin, 2005).

6 George Wharton Edwards, *Brittany and the Bretons* (New York,
1911), pp. 226–7.

7 *CIA – The World Factbook* (2012), at www.cia.gov, last accessed
21 March 2012.

8 'A Frenchman's Description of Hallowe'en', *Hogg's Instructor*
(Edinburgh, 1851), n.s. VI, p. 223–4.

9 'Halloween: An Ungodly Import', CNN.com, 31 October 2003,
at http://edition.cnn.com, last accessed 21 March 2012.

10 Parmy Olson, 'Halloween Declared Dead in France', Forbes.com,
31 October 2006, at www.forbes.com, last accessed 21 March 2012.

11 Edward Eyre Hunt, 'Ghosts', *The New Republic*, IX/115 (1917),
p. 291.

12 Po Tidholm, 'Halloween', Sweden.se (2004), at www.sweden.se,
last accessed 21 March 2012.

13 Henry Frederic Reddall, *Fact, Fancy, and Fable: A New Handbook for Ready Reference on Subjects Commonly Omitted from Cyclopaedias* (Chicago, 1892), p. 25.

14 Lothar Mikos, 'How the Pumpkins Conquered Germany: Halloween, Media and Reflexive Modernization in Germany', in *Treat or Trick?*, ed. Foley and O'Donnell, p. 128.

15 David Greene, 'Fear the Pumpkin: In Ukraine, It's the Big Kiss-off', *NPR*, 29 October 2010, at www.npr.org, last accessed 21 March 2012.

16 Chris, 'Our Halloween in Poland: The Positives and the Negatives', *Kielbasa Stories*, 1 November 2010, at http://kielbasastories.blogspot.com, last accessed 21 March 2012.

17 Allen Paul, 'Poland's Profound "Halloween"', *NewsObserver*, 30 October 2009, at www.newsobserver.com, last accessed 21 March 2012.

18 Richard Ford, *Handbook for Travellers in Spain, Part I* (London, 1855), 3rd edn, p. 208.

19 Salvador Cardús, 'Halloween: Tradition as Snobbery', from *Treat or Trick?*, ed. Foley and O'Donnell, p. 111.

20 Enric Castelló, 'Halloween in a Situation Comedy: Postmodernity, Tradition and Identity', *Treat or Trick?*, ed. Foley and O'Donnell, pp. 202–12.

21 'All Souls", *The Saturday Review*, LXV/1680 (1888), pp. 11–12.

22 E. C. Vansittart, 'All Souls' Day in Italy', *The Antiquary*, XXXVI (1900), p. 326.

23 Dmitry Sudakov, 'Halloween and other borrowed holidays make Russians forget their roots and traditions', *Pravda*, 31 October 2006, at http://english.pravda.ru, last accessed 21 March 2012.

24 'Haunted City: Moscow paints up for the scariest holiday of the year', *RT*, 29 October 2010, at http://rt.com, last accessed 21 March 2012.

25 Ibid.

26 Heather Brooke, 'Leave Your Taboos at the Gate', *The Sydney Morning Herald*, 9 December 2010, at www.smh.com.au, last accessed 21 March 2012.

27 'McCain: Purim=Halloween?', *First Read from NBC News*, 20 March 2008, at http://firstread.msnbc.msn.com, last accessed 21 March 2012.

28 Zoe Li, 'Hong Kong Halloween: Socially Acceptable Self-Indulgence', *CNNGo* (2010), at www.cnngo.com, last accessed 21 March 2012.

29 Wang Shanshan, 'Terrifying Trend: Halloween Takes Off', *China Daily*, 30 October 2006, at www.chinadaily.com.cn, last accessed 21 March 2012.

30 Sophie Hardach, 'Halloween stirs imagination in costume-loving Japan', *Reuters*, 29 October 2007, at www.reuters.com, last accessed 21 March 2012.

31 Melanie Peters, 'How Halloween Splits the Faithful', *IOL News*, 31 October 2009, at www.iol.co.za, last accessed 21 March 2012.

5 *Dias de los Muertos*

1 Mary J. Andrade, *Through the Eyes of the Soul, Day of the Dead in Mexico: Puebla, Tlaxcala, San Luis Potosi, Hidalgo* (San Jose, CA, 2002), p. 107.

2 Richard F. Townsend, *The Aztecs* (New York, 2000), p. 212.

3 Elizabeth Carmichael and Chlöe Sayer, *The Skeleton at the Feast: The Day of the Dead in Mexico* (Austin, TX, 1991), p. 28.

4 Ibid., p. 40.

5 Carl Christian Wilhelm Sartorius, *Mexico: Landscapes and Popular Sketches* (New York, 1859), p. 161.

6 Ibid., p. 163.

7 Mary J. Andrade, *Through the Eyes of the Soul, Day of the Dead in Mexico: Michoacan* (San Jose, CA, 2003), p. 34.

8 Madame Calderón de la Barca, *Life in Mexico, During a Residence of Two Years in That Country* (London, 1843), p. 371.

9 Mrs V. A. Lucier, '"Offrenda" on All Souls' Day in Mexico', *Journal of American Folk-lore*, x/36 (1897), p. 106.

10 'Feast for the Dead: A Mexican town enjoys a holiday in its graveyard', *Life*, XXVII/22 (1949), p. 36.

11 David Agren, 'Janitzio awaits huge tourist influx', *Guadalajara Reporter*, 28 October 2005, at http://guadalajarareporter.com, last accessed 21 March 2012.

12 Antonio Rodriguez, ed., *Posada: El artiste queretrató a unaépoca* (Mexico City, 1978), p. 202.

13 Mary J. Andrade, *Through the Eyes of the Soul, Day of the Dead in Mexico: Mexico City, Mixquic & Morelos* (San Jose, CA, 2003), p. 48.

14 Perry Santanachote, 'New Yorkers Celebrate El Dia de los Muertos (Day of the Dead)', *WNYC Culture*, 29 October 2010, at http://culture.wnyc.org, last accessed 21 March 2012.

15 Mark Stevenson, 'Church Slams Halloween in Mexico', *The Seattle
Times*, 31 October 2007, at http://seattletimes.nwsource.com,
last accessed 21 March 2012.

16 Ibid.

17 'Chavez Calls for Ban on Halloween', *BBC News*, 30 October 2005,
at http://news.bbc.co.uk, last accessed 21 March 2012.

6 From Burns to Burton:
Halloween and Popular Culture

1 Sir Walter Scott, ed., *Minstrelsy of the Scottish Border: Consisting of
Historical and Romantic Ballads, Collected in the Southern Counties
of Scotland; With a Few of Modern Date, Founded on Local Tradition*
(Edinburgh, 1812), vol. II, p. 198–9.

2 Robert Chambers, *The Book of Days: A Miscellany of Popular
Antiquities in Connection with the Calendar* (London and Edinburgh,
1832), vol. II, p. 520.

3 M. G. Lewis, 'Bothwell Bonny Jane', in *Tales of Wonder* (London,
1801), vol. I, p. 9.

4 Lewis, *Tales of Wonder*, p. 5.

5 Scott, *Minstrelsy of the Scottish Border*, p. 204.

6 Sir Walter Scott, *The Monastery* (London and New York, 1896),
p. 114.

7 Arthur Cleveland Coxe, *Hallowe'en, A Romaunt, with Lays,
Meditative and Devotional* (Hartford, CT, 1845), p. 11.

8 Edgar Allan Poe, 'Ulalume', in *The Poetical Works of Edgar Allan
Poe* (London, 1882), p. 32.

9 Ibid., p. 35.

10 Edgar Allan Poe, *Tales of Mystery and Imagination* (London, 1903),
p. 254.

11 Nathaniel Hawthorne, 'Young Goodman Brown', in *Mosses from
an Old Manse* (New York, 1851), p. 69.

12 Washington Irving, 'The Legend of Sleepy Hollow', in *The
Sketch-book of Geoffrey Crayon, Gent.* (Philadelphia, PA, 1835),
vol. II, p. 256 .

13 Irving, 'Rip Van Winkle', in *The Sketch-book of Geoffrey Crayon*,
vol. I, p. 52.

14 Meta G. Adams, 'Halloween, or Chrissie's Fate', *Scribner's Monthly
Magazine,* vol. III (November 1871), p. 26.

15 William Sharp, 'Halloween: A Threefold Chronicle', *Harper's New
Monthly Magazine*, LXXIII (1886), p. 852.

16 Martha Russell Orne, *Hallowe'en: How to Celebrate It* (New York, 1898), pp. 8–9.

17 Stanley Schell, *Werner's Readings and Recitations No. 31: Hallowe'en Festivities* (New York, 1903), p. 11.

18 Ibid., p. 16.

19 Ibid., p. 22.

20 Clara J. Denton, *Creepy Hallowe'en Celebrations* (Dayton, OH, 1926), p. 91.

21 Elizabeth F. Guptill, 'Her Opinion', in *Halloween Fun Book* (Chicago, IL, 1936), p. 12.

22 Dorothy M. Shipman et al., *The Jolly Hallowe'en Book* (Syracuse, NY, 1937), p. 12.

23 Frances Somers, *Minneapolis Hallowe'en Fun Book* (Minneapolis, MN, 1937), p. 5.

24 Ruth Edna Kelley, *The Book of Hallowe'en* (Boston, MA, 1919), p. vii.

25 Ibid., p. 171.

26 Ralph and Adelin Linton, *Halloween Through Twenty Centuries* (New York, 1950), p. 3, p. 5.

27 Ibid., p. 67.

28 Ibid., pp. 8, 49.

29 Ibid.

30 Ibid., p. 104.

31 Gary Shapiro, 'Studying the Academic Side of Halloween', *New York Sun*, 1 November 2006, at www.nysun.com, last accessed 21 March 2012.

32 Stuart Schneider, *Halloween in America: A Collector's Guide with Prices* (Atglen, PA, 1995), p. 15.

33 Dan and Pauline Campanelli, *Halloween Collectables: A Price Guide* (Gas City, IN, 1995), p. 5.

34 Ray Bradbury, *The Halloween Tree* (Colorado Springs, CO, 2005), p. 310.

35 Ibid., p. 469.

36 Capt. J. E. Alexander, *Transatlantic Sketches, Comprising Visits to the Most Interesting Scenes in North and South America, and the West Indies* (Philadelphia, PA, 1833), p. 311.

37 Mary D. Brine, *Elsie's Hallowe'en Experience* (New York, 1888), p. 55.

38 Richard J. Hand, '"Stay Tuned for Tricks, Treats, and Terror": Halloween and Horror Radio in the Golden Age of American Live Broadcasting', in *Treat or Trick?: Halloween in a Globalising World*, ed. Malcolm Foley and Hugh O'Donnell (Newcastle upon Tyne, 2009), p. 225.

39 Coeli Carr, 'Real Witches Cry Foul at Portrayal on "True Blood"', *Reuters*, 12 August 2011, at www.reuters.com, last accessed 21 March 2012.

40 Irving, *The Sketch-book*, vol. II, p. 237.

41 Adam Rockoff, *Going to Pieces: The Rise and Fall of the Slasher Film, 1978–1986* (Jefferson, NC, 2002), p. 53.

42 Roger Ebert, *Roger Ebert's Movie Home Companion* (New York, 1985), p. 157.

43 Kim Newman, *Nightmare Movies: A Critical Guide to Contemporary Horror Films* (New York, 1988), p. 145.

44 Rockoff, *Going to Pieces*, p. 55.

45 Mark Salisbury, ed., *Burton on Burton* (London, 2006), revd edn, p. 124.

46 Roger Ebert, 'Tim Burton's The Nightmare Before Christmas', 22 October 1993, at http://rogerebert.suntimes.com, last accessed 21 March 2012.

47 Richard Corliss, 'A Sweet and Scary Treat', *Time*, 11 October 1993, at www.time.com, last accessed 21 March 2012.

48 Joe Leydon, 'Trick 'r Treat', *Variety*, 12 October 2009, at www.variety.com, last accessed 21 March 2012.

49 Buzz, 'Review: Trick 'r Treat', CampBlood, 6 October 2009, at http://campblood.org, last accessed 21 March 2012.

50 Lesley Pratt Bannatyne, *Halloween Nation: Behind the Scenes of America's Fright Night* (Gretna, LA, 2011), p. 136.

51 'I Luv Halloween Review', *Publisher's Weekly*, 24 October 2005, at http://books.google.com, last accessed 21 March 2012.

52 A. R. Wright, *British Calendar Customs: England*, vol. III: *Fixed Festivals: June–December, Inclusive*, ed. T. E. Lones (London, 1940), p. 123.

53 Edward Barber and P. H. Ditchfield, *Memorials of Old Cheshire* (London, 1910), pp. 231.

54 Robert Holland, *A Glossary of Words used in the County of Chester* (London, 1886), pp. 506–9.

55 Sharp, 'Halloween: A Threefold Chronicle', p. 848.

56 Lenore K. Dolan, *The Best Halloween Book* (Chicago, IL, 1931), p. 147.

57 'Thriller, Halloween 2011, Kiev, Ukraine', YouTube (2011), at www.youtube.com, last accessed 21 March 2012.

58 Bannatyne, *Halloween Nation*, p. 12.

59 'Haunted Houses Now Open Beyond October', PRNewswire, 27 October 2011, at www.prnewswire.com, last accessed 21 March 2012

212

Acknowledgements

Thanks are due first to my commissioning editor at Reaktion, Ben Hayes, who approached me about this book (in what remains one of the best email treats I've ever received). I'd also like to thank Reaktion's production staff and my agent Robert Fleck.

In addition to the usual suspects – Pamela Apkarian-Russell, Lesley Bannatyne, David Bertolino, Rich Hanf, Jack Santino, Al Sarrantonio, Stuart Schneider, the staff of the Central Los Angeles Public Library, the Iliad Bookshop and Dark Delicacies – I'd also like to thank Rocky Wood for his Stephen King information, Rocky and Greg Chapman for notes on Australian festivities, and Marilyn and Damien Valentine for Guy Fawkes research. Thank you to those of you who responded to my calls for photos or kindly provided rights, including Kat Caro, Pete Dudar, Brian Freeman at Cemetery Dance Publications, Craig Knighton, Karen Romanko, Christopher Slatsky, and Scott Smith of Rucus Studios. And lastly, biggest thanks to Ricky Grove for tips on Archive.org and for invaluable support with everything.

Photo Acknowledgements

The author and publishers wish to express their thanks to the below sources of illustrative material and / or permission to reproduce it:

Photo Cemetery Dance Publications, Forest Hill, Maryland: p. 177; photos Pete Dudar: pp. 6, 194; photo Craig Knighton: p. 117; photo copyright Knott's, Buena Park, California: p. 103; private collection: p. 191; Scott Smith/Rucus Studio (photo courtesy Scott Smith): p. 192; photo ToyahAnette B.: p. 124.

Index